Life & Times Series

BREL

BRE

BRITISH RAIL ENGINEERING LIMITED

The major BREL electric multiple unit manufacturer for many years was York, with products for both the home and overseas markets being produced. The first Scottish Region Class 318 driving vehicle is seen being assembled in the main shop in February 1986.

Colin J. Marsden

Life & Times Series

BREL

BRE
BRITISH RAIL ENGINEERING LIMITED

Colin J. Marsden

Haynes

Oxford Publishing Co.

Contents

A FOULIS-OPC Railway Book

© 1990 C.J. Marsden & Haynes Publishing Group

The former BREL Eastleigh Works, now part of the British Rail Maintenance Group, was the major SR locomotive/unit overhaul facility. Class 33/0 No. 33055 is seen in the locomotive repair area on 18th September 1985, whilst receiving classified attention, including a full repaint.

Colin J. Marsden

British Library Cataloguing in Publication Data

Marsden, C. J. (Colin J)
    British Rail Engineering Ltd.
    1. Great Britain. Railway engineering industries.
    British Rail. British Rail Engineering, history
    I. Title
    338.7`6251`00941

ISBN 0-86093-440-3

Library of Congress catalog card number
89-85909

Published by:
Haynes Publishing Group
Sparkford, Near Yeovil, Somerset. BA22 7JJ

Haynes Publications Inc.
861 Lawrence Drive, Newbury Park, California 91320, USA.

Printed by: J.H. Haynes & Co. Ltd

Introduction

Interest in the railway workshops and engineering activities is quite considerable, but to most people these are rather mysterious places, often with uniformed security guards on all gates. Observation of stock and operations can usually only be from travelling on passing trains or organised party visits. Regrettably casual visits are not permitted to any of the railway engineering functions on grounds of safety.

This book has been prepared to cover all workshops that formed British Rail Engineering Limited (BREL), a business that commenced trading on 1st January 1970, following reorganisation of the British Railways Board (BRB) as legislated under Sections 48(2), and 48(4) of the 1968 Transport Act. From 1st January 1970 the BRB assumed a mainly non-executive role, directing its attention to planning, policy, and longer term direction. The day to day responsibility of running the railway being delegated to five Regional Managers (one for each region), and a Managing Director of BREL, formerly the BR Workshops Division. The establishment of BREL was undertaken to facilitate the running of the former BR controlled workshops as a commercial undertaking, not only to manufacture and repair material for BR, but where capacity and skills existed, to manufacture and repair anything from the private sector, including other nationalised industries equipment. When BREL was formed the BRB announced that it would aim to keep up an optimum workload by carrying out work for outside customers which could be done competitively at commercial prices, it was envisaged that much of this would be in miscellaneous sub-contract undertakings, such as foundry, machining, forging, spring-making, and metal fabrication.

British Rail Engineering Limited or BREL as it was more usually referred, was one of the largest engineering organisations in the country, with an annual turnover in excess of £450 million. The group's works, located throughout the country, provided heavy maintenance facilities for BR's locomotive and rolling stock fleets, together with supplying the majority of spare components used by the operating railway. A full construction service of building new locomotives, coaches, wagons, and multiple unit trains was available, and until 1985 BR purchased over 95% of its traffic fleet from the group. However, with the more competitive market of the mid-1980s the BRB decided to put all subsequent orders out on a tender basis. This meant that unless the customer (BR) were happy with the product offered the contract may well go outside the industry.

During the late 1970s and early 1980s BREL became 'train makers to the world' with their products operating in some 33 countries on all five continents. With the 1980's recession within BR, and a general decline in work from that source, BREL furthered its interests in the export field, this being demonstrated by construction of an international coach in 1984, and procurement and fulfilment of orders for both Northern Ireland Railways (NIR) and Coras Iompair Eireann (CIE), during 1986. Continuous research and development in new production methods, and marketing techniques resulted in the design and manufacture of 'new generation' rolling stock including diesel and electric multiple units, loco-hauled stock and an involvement in railbus projects. In the mid-1980s, when the BREL group still operated ten major railway works, their workforce was in excess of 29,000 staff.

Towards the end of 1985 major changes within the group were announced, this called for the splitting of the company into two distinct groups, one – formed of Crewe, Derby Locomotive, Derby Litchurch Lane, York, and the remaining Horwich Foundry, became the BREL construction business. While the other works: Wolverton, Doncaster, Eastleigh and Glasgow, became solely responsible for maintenance and took the name British Rail Maintenance Ltd (BRML). This group of works forming BRML were handed back to BR control from early 1987 operating exclusively for the maintenance of BR equipment. The BREL arm was able to tender for both BR maintenance and construction contracts as well as tender for work from the private sector.

A further major change to BREL was announced by Transport Secretary Mr Paul Channon in November 1987, when after months of speculation the official announcement came that BREL was to be privatised. This privatisation called for the four core works of Crewe, Derby Locomotive, Derby Litchurch Lane and York, to be sold as a single unit, while the remaining Horwich Foundry would be available for purchase separately. After the sell off announcement, tenders were invited from interested parties and received by BREL Headquarters during Spring 1988. An announcement was made at the end of 1988 that the Company, now trading as BREL (1988) Ltd would be sold to a consortium including senior members of BREL, Asea, Brown Boveri (Sweden) and Trafalgar House. The date of completion of sale was 18th April 1989, when the trading name became BREL Limited.

Although BREL Doncaster was transferred to BR from April 1987 the wagon operation remained with BREL until September when it was sold to RFS Industries, a company formed by a group of senior management staff of the former Doncaster Works.

This book has been prepared to take readers to each works operated as part of the original BREL group, providing a brief history of each establishment followed by a description of the workshop facilities and services offered. Each section is complemented by a number of illustrations of activities and products.

I should like to express my gratitude to the many people who have assisted in the production of this title, especially to the BREL Public Affairs Department at Derby, the Regional Photographic Units of BR, and Mr Graham Fenn for producing the layout drawings of each works.

Colin J. Marsden
Dawlish

Ashford

During 1846 the South Eastern Railway (SER) founded a workshop in the small Kent village of Ashford, mid-way between Tonbridge and Dover, and by 1848 the works had begun the production of locomotives. Situated at the south end of the village, the works steadily grew as did the route mileage of the SER. The company eventually operated its services jointly with the London, Chatham & Dover Railway (LCDR) in 1899 under the title South Eastern & Chatham Railway (SECR), which then took over responsibility for the works.

In the early years of the 20th century, Ashford Works became responsible for the manufacture of many hundreds of locomotives, coaches and goods wagons, including a number of frames and fabrications used by the SECR and later SR for electric multiple unit builds.

After the formation of the Southern Railway (SR) in 1923 the works had more widespread responsibilities, continuing its previous role alongside the other SR workshops located at Brighton, Lancing and Eastleigh.

During 1941 the SR secured a contract to construct some 1,600 12 ton mineral wagons for Persia. Ashford Works was given the build contract which was fulfilled in a staggering twelve weeks, (equating to a production rate of 133 wagons per week!). This was the first of many subsequent foreign contracts undertaken by this workshop and for many years Ashford led in Britain's rail export business.

The works had its first taste of 'modern traction' building in 1937 when three 0-6-0 diesel shunting locomotives were constructed for the Southern Railway. The modern traction interest continued at the time of Nationalisation with 1Co-Co1 prototype diesel electrics Nos 10201-10202 being built, as well as the first booster electric locomotive, later of Class 70. By mid-1948 it was decided to separate the activities at Ashford, and form two separate departments: one dealing with locomotives and the other wagons and fabrication work. Regrettably the locomotive works only remained in operation for a further 14 years, because in 1962 the British Transport Commission (BTC) decided to concentrate all locomotive operations at Eastleigh, thus terminating the locomotive era at Ashford after 114 years.

The final locomotive build contract undertaken was 26 0-6-0 diesel electric powered locomotives Nos 15211-15236, later classified Class 12 under the BR numerical classification system. Throughout the 1950s and early 1960s Ashford was responsible for the fabrication of hundreds of emu underframes, which upon completion were transported to Eastleigh for top side building.

During 1963 Ashford Works became part of the British Railway Workshop Division and shortly afterwards was awarded a contract to build nearly 250 Continental ferry vans. This order was closely followed by several BR orders for specialised freight stock, including fly-ash, car transporting, 'cartic' vehicles and subsequently the first Freightliner flats and their relevant containers. As a result of the Railway's decision to modernise its freight business a large number of high capacity merry-go-round (mgr) vehicles was also built.

Ashford Works became part of the BREL group upon the company's formation on 1st January 1970, which provided powers to undertake work for private industry, as well as fulfilling its major role of production and maintenance for its parent company British Rail.

Following the BREL takeover there was a major reorganisation of the workshop business, leading to Ashford becoming one of the two works within the group with a major responsibility for wagons. In consequence, during the early 1970s a substantial export order was placed with the works for the build of 800 covered wagons for Yugoslavian Railways. In following years further orders were received from Middle and Far Eastern countries for bogie hopper wagons and also from a British private operator for tank wagons. BR's own freight operators placed orders with BREL Ashford in the 1970s for many air-braked wagon types. By the late 1970s Ashford Works had become the BREL group's major export builder and contracts included 1,200 metre gauge wagons for Kenya Railways, 510 wagons for the Tanzania Railway Corporation, 825 vehicles for Bangladesh, and a further 750 vehicles for the British market – these being a mixture of open, ferry and bogie steel types. A major refurbishing contract on earlier BR vehicles was also undertaken by the works, as was conversion work on a number of Palvans to enable them to be used for the conveyance of British Leyland motorcar components.

After the Class 56 locomotive contract had been awarded to BREL a number of their works were given associated assembly operations, Ashford Works manufacturing the roof sections. Apart from conversion and new build contracts, Ashford Works undertook routine maintenance to revenue earning and departmental stock throughout the 1970s, as well as providing a major repair facility for wagon wheelsets.

Regrettably, due to alterations in workshop practices, declining order books and a decision to concentrate the BREL operations at fewer premises, the works at Ashford was gradually run down during the late 1970s and finally closed in 1981. All wagon and new build contracts were then concentrated at Shildon, York and Doncaster works.

During the 1970s the main works buildings were divided into the following shops:

Shot Blasting and Degreasing Shop To prolong the life of a number of components against rust, and therefore improving construction quality, most steel products passed through this shop prior to assembly and painting.

Smith and Press Shop Ashford Works housed a full blacksmith's shop with a hot-cold pressing facility. There were also sizeable furnaces for use in pressing and heat treatment operations. A flash butt-welding unit was also provided.

Diesel and Electric locomotive construction at Ashford 1937-52:

Type	Numbers	Total	Years
Diesel			
0-6-0	15201-15203	3	1937
1Co-Co1	10201-10202	2	1950-51
0-6-0	15211-15236	26	1949-52
Electric			
Co-Co	CC1-CC3	3	1941-48

Fabrication and Welding Shop It was within the confines of this shop that all major structures for new build and repairs were fabricated from plate or section. Equipment existed for arc or CO_2 welding procedures.

New Construction Shops Nos 1, 2 and 3 Although Ashford Works was comparatively small when placed against other BREL sites, it boasted three construction shops, each housing special jigs and manipulators to allow rapid item progress, high capacity overhead cranes were also provided to enable easy movement of equipment and vehicles around the shops. A flow-line construction programme was usually used but this depended upon the vehicles under construction. A stringent quality control examination was effected at the end of each production line. Having three separate construction shops permitted three individual building programmes to operate simultaneously.

Medium Machine Shop This small facility situated adjacent to two of the construction shops, housed power cutting and milling equipment, in addition to a multi-head flame cutter, used in the initial preparation of steel plate. A levelling press was also incorporated for straightening fabricated underframes. Drilling equipment jigs were also provided in this shop.

Paint Shop Running almost the full length of the main buildings was a paint shop where all finished products passed for cosmetic attention prior to despatch. One section of this shop was set aside for sign-writing, while another was used for the production of silk screens for wagon numbering and lettering.

Apart from the 'major' shops within the main works building, other smaller out-buildings were positioned around the complex, these included:

The Wheel Shop Here assembly, machining and maintenance of wheelsets was effected, this included an amount of private owner work for the growing private owner wagon fleet, together with a small quantity of export work.

Sub-assembly Shop Here many small component sub-assemblies were formed prior to transport to the main construction shop.

Heavy Machine Shop This housed the shaping, slotting, milling and grinding machinery. Material movements within the shop being effected by a high capacity overhead crane.

Light Machine Shop This small shop carried out all machining of components for new construction and repair contracts, the main equipment included a milling, turning and small shaping press. One part of this shop was set aside for the tin-smith's work.

Shear Shop All raw materials arriving on the works passed through this building where they were sheared to size before passing to other shops.

Apart from the usual office complex, located adjacent to the main works building, there was also a sizeable works training school, canteen and first aid facilities.

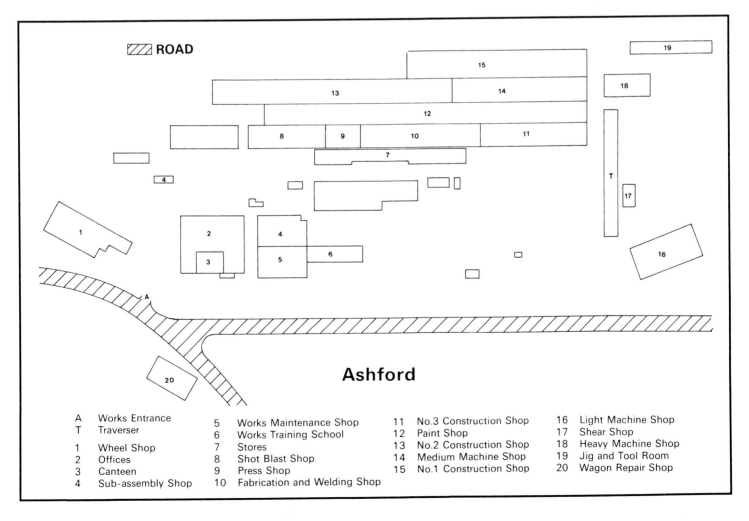

Ashford

A	Works Entrance	5	Works Maintenance Shop	11	No.3 Construction Shop	16	Light Machine Shop
T	Traverser	6	Works Training School	12	Paint Shop	17	Shear Shop
1	Wheel Shop	7	Stores	13	No.2 Construction Shop	18	Heavy Machine Shop
2	Offices	8	Shot Blast Shop	14	Medium Machine Shop	19	Jig and Tool Room
3	Canteen	9	Press Shop	15	No.1 Construction Shop	20	Wagon Repair Shop
4	Sub-assembly Shop	10	Fabrication and Welding Shop				

General view of the main construction shop which was one of the longest at any works, being nearly 1/4 mile long. This shop consisted of two tracked production lines with a central area for small items of immediate stores. When this picture was taken on 22nd November 1977 the final stage of a 1,200-vehicle wagon contract for Kenya was being completed.

When vehicle frames were fabricated, the completed assembly was normally rotated by a manipulator enabling easy all-round access for staff. A Kenyan wagon underframe is seen installed in a manipulator on the left, while a complete frame lies on the workshop floor to the right.

During the 1970s Ashford was the major contributor to the BREL export drive, with a considerable number of wagons being produced for foreign railway administrations. Here four bogie vans forming part of a Yugoslavian contract near completion during November 1973.

Two completed Ashford export products stand in the works yard awaiting despatch to their owners. The upper illustration shows a bogie flat wagon assembled for Kenya, while the lower illustration shows a top loading phosphate hopper wagon constructed as part of an order for the Aqaba Railway Corporation of Jordan.

In days long prior to BREL's operation of the works, locomotive construction was effected for the Southern Railway. Here, Bulleid designed 0-6-0 350hp diesel electric shunter No. 15228 takes shape in the main erecting shop during early 1951.

Les Elsey

The two pioneering Southern main line diesel electric locomotives, Nos 10201 and 10202 were both constructed at Ashford Works. In this view the completed body shell of No. 10201 is seen in the main erecting shop. The engine compartment roof hatches are seen in the open position, while adjacent to the locomotive is the steam heat boiler awaiting installation.

Author's Collection

Crewe

This works originated in 1843 as the construction and repair facility for the Grand Junction Railway (GJR) and was, in the latter years of BREL's reign, the most important factory within the group. The works were situated to the north east of the town's station and adjacent to the Crewe-Chester line, and during 1987 the complex occupied some 90 acres of prime Cheshire countryside.

As previously mentioned, the GJR first decided to concentrate their operation at Crewe in 1843, when the Company occupied a miniscule 2¹/₂ acre site with just two buildings – one dealing with carriages and wagons, and the other locomotives. This site gradually expanded and was later taken over by the London & North Western Railway (LNWR), and subsequently by the London Midland & Scottish Railway (LMSR) in 1923. During the 1930s, when the railways were in their hey-day, the Crewe Works complex occupied some 136 acres, of which over 40 acres were covered buildings.

Between 1845, when the first steam locomotive was constructed, and December 1958, when the last steam locomotive – Class 9F 2-10-0 No. 92250 was completed, a total well in excess of 7,000 steam locomotives had been built at Crewe.

Crewe's association with the modern traction era commenced in 1957 when a batch of the ubiquitous 0-6-0 diesel electric shunters (now Class 08) were constructed. The modern traction programme continued with only a few breaks until the late 1980s with diesel electrics, diesel hydraulics, electro-diesels, IC125 power cars and electric locomotives all being constructed.

Modern traction construction at Crewe since 1957:

Type	Class	Total	Years
–	08	135	1957-60
2	24	54	1959-60
4	45	105	1960-62
4	47	202	1964-67
4	52	44	1962-63
5	56	20	1983-84
Electro-Diesel			
4	74 +	10	1967-68
Electric			
5	87	36	1973-74
5	89	1	1985
5	90*	50	1987-90
5	91*	31	1988-90
IC125			
4	252(41)	2	1972
4	253/4(43)	197	1976-82

+ Conversion from Class 71.
* Still in progress of delivery.

A significant milestone in Crewe's railway workshop history was reached in February 1978 when IC125 power car No. 43081 was constructed, this being the 8,000th powered vehicle assembled at Crewe. This figure demonstrated that on average one new locomotive had been produced at the works each week since 1843.

After being taken over by the BTC in 1948 and operated under the Workshop Division's flag, by the mid-1960s it was foreseen that Crewe Works was in need of a major facelift and reorganisation to bring it into line with modern requirements. To fulfil this, refurbishment commenced during 1964 and took over four years to complete at a cost of some £2 million. The work included the rationalisation of both land and buildings and the concentration of the works on a 90 acre site. However 40 acres were still covered factory, stores and offices.

During the 1930s Crewe Works employed in excess of 20,000 people and was at that time the largest employer in the County of Cheshire. However, following the mid-1960's alterations and considerable rationalisation of staff in the ensuing years, during 1986 the employment figure at the works stood around 3,500.

In common with the majority of BR workshops, Crewe came under the control of British Rail Engineering Ltd with effect from 1st January 1970. Initially this change did not affect the day to day operation at the works but progressively alterations were made to the workload.

Although the most well-known aspect of Crewe Works has, in recent years, been the repair and maintenance of main line diesel and electric locomotives, a number of other important activities have also been undertaken. These included the manufacture and maintenance of point and signal equipment, including signal gantries, the manufacture of coach and wagon springs, and the repair and testing of specialised lifting tackle. BREL Crewe Works also had a steel foundry, the only one latterly within the group, supplying castings to other BREL Works in addition to a number of BR depots.

Until 1989 it was usual for the Crewe Works complex to have around 60 main line locomotives on hand at any one time, these receiving either casual or classified overhauls. By early 1989 it had become apparent at Crewe that BR's Cost Effective Maintenance policy was drastically affecting input to the works, with only a handful of main line locomotives being resident. One of the more recent achievements at the works has been the construction of Class 90 and 91 locomotives, in the latter case BREL acting as chief sub-contractor to GEC Transportation Ltd. In addition to the above, one of the main activities at the works in recent years was the dismantling of many withdrawn locomotives. This has included many members of the Class 40 fleet and the first inroads into the Class 47s, but this work has now ceased.

Following the privatisation of BREL, under the name of BREL Ltd in 1989, Crewe Works saw a further drastic reduction in locomotive work with, at the time of privatisation, the workload largely consisting of construction of Class 90 and 91 electric locomotives, and the commencement of coach shell construction.

During 1987 the works was formed of the following main shops:

Diesel & Electric Locomotive Repair Shop This housed the main hub of works activity and it is where all diesel and electric locomotives have been latterly repaired.

There were facilities for bogies to be removed, bodies and underframes to be cleaned and body repair work to be carried out if required, as well as general reconstruction work. Following the dismantling process, all repairable components were taken to other shops within the works for attention. New building programmes, particularly those of the IC125 fleet and the Class 56s were carried out in this shop. Within this area a number of traversers were provided to enable locomotives to be moved road to road without being lifted. In addition overhead gantry cranes were provided.

Within this area a number of traversers were provided to enable locomotives to be moved road to road without being lifted. In addition overhead gantry cranes were provided.

Power Unit & Bogie Repair Shop Running parallel to the Diesel & Electric Locomotive Repair Shop was this area with facilities to strip, repair and reassemble all power units. Full bench test equipment was provided to enable pre-installation testing to be effected. Power units and bogies that were replaced on depots were also repaired at Crewe, these being either despatched back to a depot for further use or used within the works.

Main Machine Shop This sizeable shop was parallel to the Power Unit & Bogie Repair Shop, manufacturing and assembling the majority of items used in the construction, maintenance and repair of locomotives. The shop was equipped with some of the most modern electronically controlled drilling and milling machines, together with a number of capstan lathes. This shop also undertook repair work to locomotive brake gear, vacuum exhausters, air compressors and turbo chargers. A special 'clean room' was provided for fuel pump and fuel injector overhauls, as these items had to be maintained in the highest standard of cleanliness. Adjacent to the shop was a tool room producing most items of works tooling and jigs.

Locomotive Test Centre One of the most important activities following either construction or repair was thorough testing. For this a 7-road test centre, with four control rooms having the capacity to test seven locomotives simultaneously. To provide sound insulation, 20ft high sound protection booms were erected either side of the test centre. In addition to works testing, 'active' test trains were normally operated by each locomotive prior to release to traffic.

Paint Shop This long building located near the Goddard Street entrance carried out all body preparation, paint and cosmetic attention to locomotives prior to release into service. The shop was modernised in recent years and was previously the cubicle repair and wheel shop.

Fabrication/New Build Shop Within this shop all new locomotive shells and major components were first assembled from raw steel. A number of purpose-built jigs and special tooling items were provided. From 1987 this shop was deployed on the construction of Class 90 and Class 91 second generation AC electric locomotives.

Motor Repair Shop This shop was divided into two sections, one dealing with traction motor repairs, and the other auxiliary machines. In the traction motor department locomotive alternators and generators were stripped down, serviced and reassembled. A special facility existed for the overhaul of wheel roller bearings. The auxiliary machine department carried out repairs and tests to all auxiliary electric equipment from diesel and electric locomotives, including armatures, stator windings and coils.

Copper Shop All locomotive and auxiliary machine pipework as well as sheet metal components were dealt with in this area.

Heavy Machine Shop All major assemblies and fabrications were taken to this shop for machining and drilling. High capacity overhead cranes and all modern sophisticated floor mounted machines were installed.

Steel Foundry During the early 1980s BREL had only one steel foundry, located at Crewe, this being responsible for steel castings for locomotives, carriages and wagons, together with some private sector work. The foundry was equipped with two 4 ton electric arc furnaces and fitted with the usual foundry tooling.

Wheel Shop This shop was equipped for the manufacture and repair of all types of wheel-set. Facilities included the ability to machine axles, fit axles to wheel rims, install tyres and dynamic balancing of the finished product.

Bogie Repair Shop The Bogie Repair Shop was equipped with a progressive repair system for stripping, cleaning and the overhaul of diesel and electric locomotive bogies. New bogies were also assembled in this shop.

In addition to the main shops described above there were a number of smaller works facilities dealing with signal repairs, brass work and chain repairs, all of which were a hive of constant activity. A sizeable works maintenance section was provided as well as a number of stores located at different points around the works. Staff welfare was well looked after at Crewe with a large canteen being provided, as well as medical and social care. All administration for the works was carried out in a large modern office block located by the Park entrance off West Street.

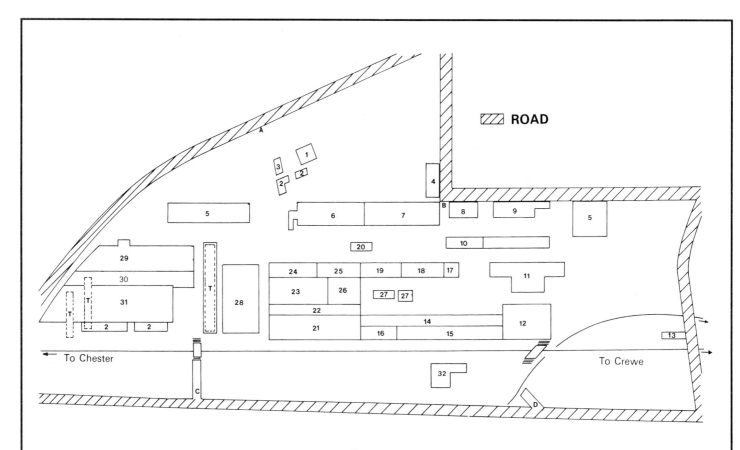

Crewe

A Main Works Entrance (West Street)
B Works Entrance (Goddard Street)
C Works Entrance (Park Huts)
D Works Entrance (Wistaston Road)
T Traverser

1 BREL House
2 Offices
3 Medical Centre
4 Works Canteen
5 Locomotive Stores

6 Works Maintenace Shop
7 Bogie Shop
8 Signal Shop
9 Brass Shop
10 New Paint Shop
11 Steel Foundry
12 Dismantling Shop
13 Welding School
14 Welding and Plate Shop
15 Chain and Smithy Shop
16 Sheet Metal Shop
17 Steam Generator Shop
18 Heavy Machine Shop
19 Copper Shop
20 Asbestos Shop
21 Fabrication Shop (Erecting)
22 Bogie and Wheel Shop
23 Erecting Shop
24 Traction Motor Repair Shop
25 Auxiliary Motor Repair Shop
26 Spring Shop
27 Boiler Plant
28 Locomotive Test Centre
29 Main Machine Shop
30 Power Unit Repair Shop
31 Diesel and Electric Locomotive
    Repair Shop
32 Training School

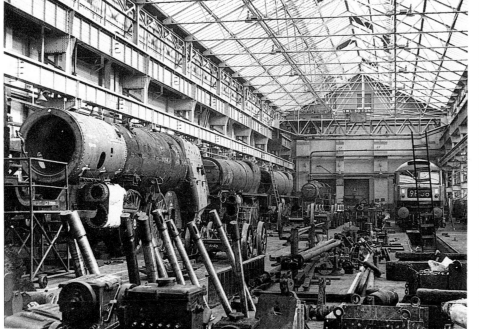

This picture, showing both steam and diesel, was taken long before the formation of BREL, when the works was under the control of the BTC Workshops Division. In this view a 'Britannia' Pacific and three Stanier Class 5s share floor space with a Brush Type 4.

J. B. Mounsey

Taken from the roof of the Diesel Locomotive Repair Shop in 1964, this illustration shows some of the major rebuilding undertaken around this period. In the foreground is the main traverser, and behind, the Locomotive Test Centre in the process of construction. Various English Electric Type 4 locomotives can be seen in the yard, together with an English Electric Type 1, a Metro-Vick Co-Bo and Brush Type 4s in various stages of repair or construction.

The Locomotive Testing Centre had seven bays, each being able to put a main line locomotive through its paces simultaneously. In this view, taken during the mid-1960s, diesel shunter No. D3068 hauls English Electric Type 4 No. D340 out of the Test Centre and onto the traverser, while sister locomotive No. D339 and two Brush Type 4s pose in other test bays.

Of all the workshops, Crewe was always able to accommodate the most number of locomotives at any given time, often being recorded as having upwards of 60 on the premises. In this splendid view taken inside the Diesel Locomotive Repair Shop during 1974, no fewer than twelve Class 47s and three Class 50s can be seen.

During 1966/67 Crewe Works was awarded a major rebuilding contract to gut and refit ten SR straight electric locomotives of Class 71 into electro-diesel locomotives of Class 74. The work was not just a simple strip and reassembly job, but every item, including side walls and cabs, were removed, modified and then replaced, thus making the rebuilding work more costly than if new locomotives had been built. Five 'ED' rebuilds can be seen inside Crewe Electric Traction Shop in this view, the almost completed example in the foreground being No. E6101.

Author's Collection

A fully equipped Heavy Machine Shop was situated adjacent to the Power Unit/Locomotive Repair Shop, being capable of undertaking virtually any machining operation required. A numerically controlled drilling machine with a Ferranti tape control unit is shown.

Hot molten steel is poured from an overhead crucible into a mould in the works steel foundry. The foundry was equipped with two 4 ton electric arc furnaces supplying steel castings to various workshops and maintenance depots.

A sizeable Bogie & Wheel Shop was provided dealing with wheel sets for stock under repair at the works. In addition the shop provided repair facilities for regional requirements. Four ac electric locomotive wheel sets stand on specially raised tracks in the Bogie Shop.

Colin J. Marsden

It is usual for complete bogies to arrive at the works for repair, either fitted to locomotives or 'shipped' in from regional locations by wagon. The repairs normally necessitate the bogie being completely dismantled, repaired and then reassembled. This illustration shows a repaired bogie being reassembled, with the bogie frame being lowered onto the wheel sets.

The Traction & Auxiliary Motor Shops carried out all necessary overhauls to main, auxiliary and heating generators, traction motors and auxiliary electrically driven machines. This picture shows a general view of the shop with generators receiving attention on the left, and traction motors towards the middle of the shop.

Running full length along one side of the Diesel Locomotive Repair Shop was the power unit repair area. Here units were placed on works accommodation stands, stripped, repaired and reassembled. The top illustration shows a power unit from a Class 20 receiving attention, while the lower picture shows a Class 37 unit stripped down ready for reassembly.

Both: Colin J. Marsden

Following the decision to transfer construction of the final 20 Class 56s from Doncaster to Crewe, a huge amount of stores had to be transferred between the two works. Here two cooler groups stand in the Power Unit Repair Shop, together with various power unit components after arrival from Doncaster.

Colin J. Marsden

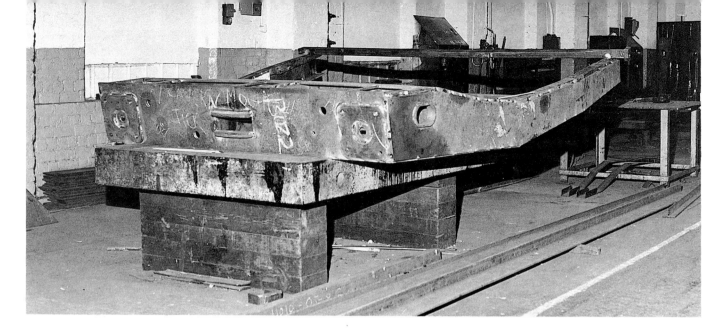

The Fabrication Shop was responsible for the formation of all large metal assemblies and constructing the basic frames of locomotives before handing them to the New Build Shop. A fabricated Class 56 dragbox awaits detail completion in the Fabrication Shop on 6th April 1982. The position for the coupling and buffers having already been made.

Colin J. Marsden

During 1972/74 BREL Crewe undertook the construction of 36 Class 87 locomotives introduced primarily for Anglo-Scottish services on the WCML. Locomotive No. 87001, the first of the build, takes shape in the Electric Locomotive Shop during late 1972.

In the period June 1972 to August 1982 BREL Crewe constructed 199 InterCity 125 power cars, providing an average of one car being completed every 18 working days! The last power car of the build, No. 43198 is seen in the Main Erecting Shop soon after delivery from the fabricators.

Colin J. Marsden

Similar to a big jigsaw where all the pieces 'just' fit together, a completed body fabrication for Class 56 No. 56118 stands inside the Fabrication Shop awaiting a set of accommodation bogies to transfer it to the Erecting Shop. Unlike Doncaster, where body panels were applied at the fabrication stage, the Crewe products were panelled during assembly.

Colin J. Marsden

After the IC125 power cars were physically completed there followed a major testing period. This was first carried out in part of the Construction Shop and later in one of the berths of the Test Centre. This test procedure culminated in a stringent 'active' road test. Power car No. 43190 poses in undercoat awaiting final testing.

Colin J. Marsden

1985/86 saw the construction of the prototype Class 89 locomotive, this being a joint venture between Brush Electrical Machines and BREL. In this illustration the body shell is seen taking shape in the Main Erecting Shop some 18 months prior to the locomotive being completed.

Colin J. Marsden

The most common visitor to BREL Crewe Works was the Class 47, with for many years around 25 'on works' at any one time. No. 47901 fitted experimentally with a Class 58 power unit receives its new heart in the former Electric Repair Shop in 1979. This locomotive was previously fitted with a Class 56 power unit for equipment evaluation when the running number applied was 47601, as still carried here.

Colin J. Marsden

When locomotives were technically complete they normally passed to the Paint Shop where bodies were de-greased, filled, rubbed down, undercoated and finally given a top coat of paint. Following this the locomotive passed to the test section. Class 47 No. 47541 receives detail finishing on 6th April 1982 in the old Paint Shop.
Colin J. Marsden

Upon arrival at the works a detailed examination was carried out on each locomotive establishing the extent of necessary repair and the subsequent costing. After this the locomotive would be stripped of all components for overhaul. The basic shell of Class 47 No. 47214 is seen in the main stripping area.

Colin J. Marsden

To avoid water or dirt from entering the delicate interior of a 25kV electric locomotive with its roof removed, large plastic sheets are seen tied over the body of Class 86/3 No. 86322. This locomotive was modified to a Class 86/4 whilst at the works emerging as No. 86422.

Colin J. Marsden

With an ex-works set of AC electric locomotive wheels in the foreground Class 86/2 No. 86259 *Peter Pan* receives an intermediate overhaul in this view of the Electric Locomotive Repair Shop taken in April 1982. During subsequient alterations at the works this shop became the main wheel maintenance area.

Colin J. Marsden

To the front of the main Locomotive Construction & Maintenance Centre was a locomotive preparation apron where completed locomotives were fuelled, oiled and watered, and then high voltage tested. Class 47 Nos 47050 and 47229 in company with Class 37 No. 37099, are shown in this area.

Colin J. Marsden

After receiving only casual attention, Class 47/4 No. 47543 awaits its turn on the Locomotive Test Centre prior to returning to traffic. Note the old brazier in front of the locomotive, an item left behind from the steam age perhaps?

Colin J. Marsden

With the BRB's decision to change the corporate livery of many locomotives and coaches, Crewe Works was obliged to amend a number of schemes on many locomotives as they have passed through the establishment for classified attention. Painted in the interim or 'more yellow' livery Class 47/4 No. 47450 stands in the works yard during September 1984 awaiting return to traffic.

Colin J. Marsden

From 1985 one of the major operations at Crewe was the refurbishing of part of the Class 37 fleet. The work involved was extensive with the works authority considering the contract on par with a new build scheme. ETH fitted examples (Class 37/4) all emerging in 'more yellow' livery, and renumbered in the 374xx series. No. 37405 is illustrated awaiting transfer to Scotland.

Colin J. Marsden

Following the alterations at Crewe in the early 1980s, which led to the closure of the Electric Locomotive Repair Shop, 25kV ac electric locomotives have received their overhauls in the main repair building. Here Class 86/2 No. 86252 *The Liverpool Daily Post* is seen in InterCity colours nearing completion.

Colin J. Marsden

For the duration of the Class 37 refurbishing scheme it was not uncommon to find some 10-15 examples of the class receiving modernisation at one time. This general view of the main Repair Shop shows no fewer than six locomotives.

Colin J. Marsden

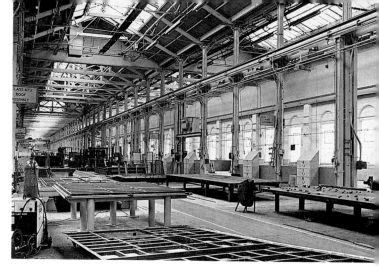

In 1987/88 one of the main works activities was the new build programme for Class 90 (originally Class 87/2) and Class 91 locomotives. This general view of the Fabrication Shop shows the two parallel construction lines for Class 87/2 (90) on the left and Class 91 on the right.

Colin J. Marsden

The first Class 87/2 (90) was bodily completed during the summer of 1987, however due to protracted fitting out the locomotive did not take to the road for trials until the late autumn. In this view of the New Build Shop, taken during the Works Open Day on 4th July 1987, No. 90001 awaits the fitting of the cab end panelling.

Colin J. Marsden

General view inside the Fabrication New Build Shop showing Class 91 No. 91002 during the advance stages of body assembly. During the course of building the Class 90 and 91 locomotives the works operated on a principle of constructing seven locomotives as a batch at the same time.

Colin J. Marsden

It is always sad to see locomotives being dismantled, however for economic reasons a proportion of the Class 47 fleet were made redundant during the mid-1980s. After all reclaimable items had been removed the body shells were dismantled in the Crewe Melt Shop. Class 47 No. 47529 is seen being dismantled on 9th April 1987.

Brian Morrison

With reorganisation of maintenance schedules Crewe Works became responsible for some Class 56 classified overhauls towards the end of 1986. After receiving its intermediate overhaul No. 56090 painted in revised Railfreight livery, stands in the main Erecting Shop in the company of Class 85 No. 85034 on 9th April 1987.

Brian Morrison

In the autumn of 1987 Crewe Works Asbestos Shop was given a surprise operation, to strip the asbestos lining out of several Scottish allocated Class 26/0s, an operation that should have already been carried out by BREL Glasgow several years before but had not been done. Therefore Crewe had to take this workload on board to fulfil a previous contract with the Company. Locomotives Nos 26014 and 26010 stand in the work's yard on 31st October 1987 awaiting admittance to the Asbestos Shop.

Brian Morrison

Derby Litchurch Lane

Derby is the only city or town in the country to have boasted two BREL establishments. Railway workshops first came to Derby in 1840 when the Midland Railway (MR) built a workshop on the site of the later Locomotive Works, which at the time of its opening dealt with locomotives, coach and wagon stock. However by 1876 the growth of the carriage and wagon business led to the Midland Railway purchasing a sizeable site in the junction between the Derby-Burton and Derby-Trent lines, which later was to become the site of Derby Litchurch Lane Works.

In the early years of the 20th century many thousands of vehicles were constructed at Litchurch Lane, the most numerous type being the open mineral wagon. In 1923 the works came under the control of the London Midland & Scottish Railway (LMS) and continued in the production of vehicle stock. About the same time as coming under the LMS flag the order books became so full that a 'flow-line' construction system was adopted – the first at any British railway workshop – capable of producing up to ten finished wagons each working day.

Between 1923 and 1948 the works was solely employed on the building and maintenance of LMS wagons and coaches. Additionally, some War Department (WD) work was undertaken during the 1940s, including the building of a number of specialised vehicles and mineral wagons.

Although taken over by the British Transport Commission in 1948 following railway nationalisation, little change came to the works until the mid-1950s when vast areas of the complex were re-equipped to cater for the modernisation plan dmu construction. 1,322 vehicles were constructed at the works between 1953 and 1960.

DMU vehicle construction, 1953-60:

Number Range	Total	Type	Year
50000	1	DMBS	1956
50001-50049	49	DMBS	1956
50050-50091	42	DMBS	1957
50092-50133	42	DMS	1957
50599-50629	31	DMBS	1958
50630-50649	17	DMC(L)	1958
50818-50870	53	DMBS	1957
50871-50923	53	DMS	1957
50938-50987	49	DMBS	1959
50988-51007	20	DMS	1958
51128-51140	13	DMBS	1958
51141-51153	13	DMS	1958
51154-51173	20	DMBS	1958
51416-51424	9	DMBS	1960
51561-51572	12	DMC(L)	1959
51591-51650	59	DMBS	1959
51651-51680	30	DMBS	1960
51849-51900	52	DMBS	1960
51901-51950	50	DMBS	1960
51985-52010	26	DMBS	1960
52011-52036	26	DMC(L)	1960
52037-52065	29	DMC(L)	1960
56000-56049	50	DTC(L)	1956
56190-56215	26	DTC(L)	1958
56221-56279	58	DTC(L)	1959
56484-56504	21	DTC(L)	1960
59000-59031	32	TC	1957
59032-59041	10	TS	1957
59245-59250	6	TBS(L)	1958
59326-59376	51	TC	1957
59380-59390	11	TS(L)	1958
59438-59448	11	TC	1958
59449-59468	20	TS	1958
59589-59618	30	TS(L)	1959
59619-59663	44	TS	1959
59664-59678	15	TC(L)	1960
59713-59718	6	TS	1960
59719-59724	6	TC(L)	1960
59725-59744	20	TS	1960
59745-59764	20	TC(L)	1960
59782-59807	26	TS(L)	1960
79000-79007	8	DMBS	1953
79008-79046	39	DMBS	1954
79118-79149	32	DMBS(L)	1955
79150-79154	5	DMS	1955
79169-79180	13	DMBS	1956
79184-79188	5	DMBS	1956
79189-79193	5	DMC(L)	1956
79250-79262	13	DTC(L)	1955
79325-79329	5	TBS(L)	1955
79400-79404	5	TS(L)	1955
79508-79512	5	DMC	1955
79600-79625	26	DTC(L)	1954
79900-79901	2	DMBS	1956

2nd Generation DMU construction 1981-88:

Class	Total (Sets)	Formation	Years
210	1	3-car	1981
210	1	4-car	1981
140	1	2-car	1981
141*	20	2-car	1983/4
142*	96	2-car	1985/6
144+	23	2-car	1986/8
144+	23	1-car	1987/8

*Bodies by Leyland.   + Bodies by Alexander.

In addition to the dmu construction detailed above the works assembled several 4-wheel Railbus vehicles during the early 1980s for evaluation in both this country and overseas.

As well as constructing diesel powered passenger vehicles, Litchurch Lane has also been responsible for a smaller number of emu vehicles.

EMU Construction 1939-1988:

Class	Total (Cars)	Years
502	152	1939-41
310	200	1966-67
423(VEP)	40*	1967-68
370(APT)	38	1979-80
317	72*	1981-87
442	120	1987-88

* Part sets only

Additional to the above dmu/emu builds the Derby works has been responsible for a high proportion of carriage stock construction in this country, this has included vast numbers of Mk I, Mk II, and the complete build of Mk IIIs. In 1989 the works involvement with coaching stock continued with the assembly of Driving Van Trailers and body construction of Mk IV vehicles.

In common with a number of railway workshops, Litchurch Lane was extensively modernised and fully re-equipped during the mid-1960s in readiness for the projected large replacement of vast numbers of coaching and good vehicles. 1964 saw the first integral design coach constructed and in 1971 work commenced on the construction of air conditioned Mk II stock. This re-shaping of the coaching stock fleet continued for many years, culminating in the production of Mk III locomotive hauled and IC125 trailer vehicles. In the early 1980s replacement for existing MkI sleeping car stock was authorised with Litchurch Lane producing 206 replacement vehicles based on established Mk III design.

With the projected replacement of many diesel unit types during the 1980s, Litchurch Lane produced two 'prototype' sets in 1981, classified 210. However, after much deliberation the design was not accepted. From 1983 Litchurch Lane was awarded the final assembly contract for Class 141, 142 and 144 Railbuses, where body shells were prefabricated by either British Leyland or Walter Alexander and transported to Derby by road for BREL completion. Other interesting projects undertaken by the works have included the APT trailer vehicles, together with a considerable number of export passenger coaches. With BREL's keen interest in the export field, an International coach was designed and built in 1984, being of modular construction easily adaptable to any operating contingency. In 1985-86 a 10-vehicle rake of BR profile International coaches was built by BREL and operated on BR for evaluation purposes.

The first complete emu sets constructed at the works for more than 20 years started to emerge in December 1987 when the first of 24 new "Wessex Electric" units, classified 442, was handed over to Network SouthEast.

Apart from the building operations at Litchurch Lane, classified overhauls on loco-hauled stock, IC125 trailer vehicles, selected dmu cars and a small amount of service wagon stock were undertaken throughout the 1980s. During 1987 the works occupied a site of some 104 acres and had a staff of around 3,500.

In 1987 the following main shops formed Derby Litchurch Lane Works. The same year the works was re-named by BREL as Derby Carriage Works.

Vehicle Building Shop This building was equipped with a continuous coach construction flowline. Body shells travelling along the shop in stages on a twin production line. Work carried out included anti-corrosion spraying, floor installation, polyurethane foam filling, installation of air conditioning modules and the general fitting out of vehicle interiors.

Lifting & Erecting Shop This shop was equipped for the progressive building of coach body shells together with integral underframes. The shop also handled repairs to some diesel unit stock, IC125 and loco-hauled passenger vehicles. Upon arrival, all vehicle bodies were removed from their bogies and any necessary repairs to the undersides effected. After these repairs, including the replacement of engines on dmu stock, vehicles were moved to the Vehicle Building Shop for reassembly.

Machine & Fitting Shop Within this shop, turning, drilling, planing, milling and grinding operations were effected. Fully automatic equipment was widely used in addition to some of the older style machinery. A staggering 15,000 items could be machined in this Shop on an average working day. Wheelsets were also assembled within the confines of this building for both Litchurch Lane and other Work's usage. One section of the building had a cold press facility for steel panels, while another was provided as a tool room for the manufacture and maintenance of jigs and works fixtures.

Paint Shop There were two Paint Shops at Litchurch Lane, one in the main area of the Works and the other at the North end. The main shop carried out all cosmetic attention to vehicles and wagons prior to release, painting being effected by hand using either the brush or roller technique. One section of the Paint Shop was used for minor Mk III vehicle repairs.

Plastics Shop The use of plastics and fibreglass within the railway industry considerably increased in the early 1980s, with this Shop producing doors, ceilings panels, pelmets, roof and gangway ends. Many items produced in this shop were supplied to BR Regional Depots.

Coach Testing After new vehicles had been completed, or existing vehicles repaired, a detailed testing of all fittings had to be made; this included brake, heating, air conditioning and electrical fitments. At one end of the shop there was a sheet metal area. DMU vehicles were tested in a special Test House near the Main Entrance.

Detail Shop This shop sheared all sheet steel to size and press-formed it into shape for constructional or repair operations. Large rotary manipulators were provided to move the sizeable fabrications.

Electric Shop The responsibility for the installation and maintenance of lighting, heating, air-conditioning units, electro-pneumatic control equipment, dynamos and alternators was placed with this shop. There was also a laboratory for repairing and testing of second-hand components.

Wagon Repair Shop The repair of wagons at Litchurch Lane declined considerably in recent years with only a few service or special plant vehicles receiving attention. As the wagon workload was light the shop catered for NPCCS repairs and a small amount of bogie overhaul.

In addition to the above main activity areas the following Shops were also provided: Asbestos Removal Plant, Finishing Shop, Polishing Shop, Trimming Shop, Brass Shop, Welding Shop, Blacksmith Shop and Buffer Shop.

A number of special supplies and stores areas were provided throughout the complex together with a well stocked Welfare & Social Club, Medical Centre and sizeable purpose-built Training School.

Following the completion of the international coach (to European loading gauge) a building was constructed near the Training School to form a Showroom for this unique vehicle.

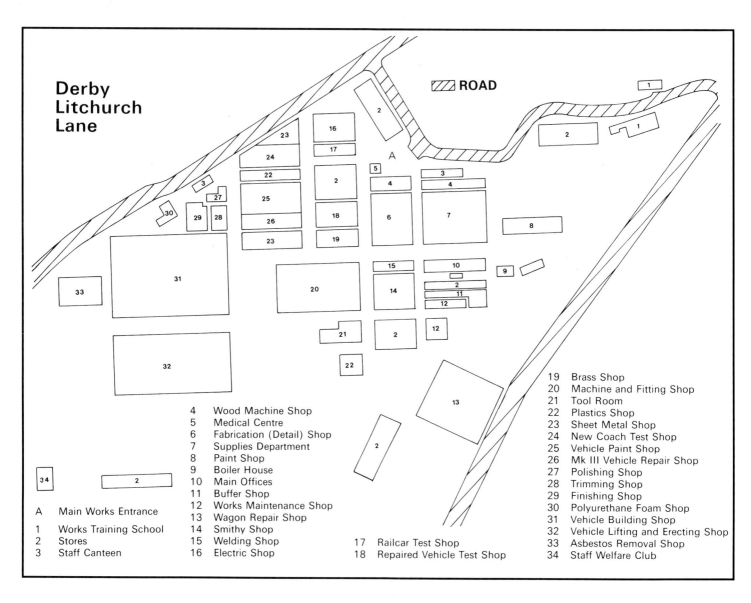

Derby Litchurch Lane

ROAD

A Main Works Entrance

A	Main Works Entrance
1	Works Training School
2	Stores
3	Staff Canteen
4	Wood Machine Shop
5	Medical Centre
6	Fabrication (Detail) Shop
7	Supplies Department
8	Paint Shop
9	Boiler House
10	Main Offices
11	Buffer Shop
12	Works Maintenance Shop
13	Wagon Repair Shop
14	Smithy Shop
15	Welding Shop
16	Electric Shop
17	Railcar Test Shop
18	Repaired Vehicle Test Shop
19	Brass Shop
20	Machine and Fitting Shop
21	Tool Room
22	Plastics Shop
23	Sheet Metal Shop
24	New Coach Test Shop
25	Vehicle Paint Shop
26	Mk III Vehicle Repair Shop
27	Polishing Shop
28	Trimming Shop
29	Finishing Shop
30	Polyurethane Foam Shop
31	Vehicle Building Shop
32	Vehicle Lifting and Erecting Shop
33	Asbestos Removal Shop
34	Staff Welfare Club

A general view of Derby Litchurch Lane Works from the Railway Technical Centre on 16th September 1989. Note the LMS research building in the foreground.

Colin J. Marsden

During 1965, prior to the Works being operated by BREL, Litchurch Lane produced the AM10, now Class 310 emus, for the LMR electrification programme. A driving vehicle of unit No. 065 is slowly pulled onto the traverser by a chain and capstan in this picture taken on 10th August 1965.

In recent years Litchurch Lane has been significantly involved in the final assembly of Leyland/Alexander Class 141, 142 and 144 Railbus vehicles. The bodies for these were produced at either Leyland Buses of Workington, or Alexanders of Dunfermline, and transferred to Derby for final fitting to BREL underframes. Class 142 No. 142008, painted in Greater Manchester PTE orange is seen near completion.

Colin J. Marsden

A general view taken to the rear of the Main Works, showing part of the steel storage area. The 15 ton capacity overhead crane, fitted with a lifting frame, is capable of unloading the stores from rail wagons or positioning commodities on trolley flats for transfer into the Works' buildings.

For a number of years Freightliner containers for both BR and the private sector were produced at this Works, but alas in more recent years this function was no longer performed. Here two craftsmen prepare timber flooring for a new build privately owned container.

Most people consider Litchurch Lane undertook only coach repairs but this was most certainly not the case as a number of NPCCS and freight vehicles were always dealt with. An FVV Motorail flat is seen supported on accommodation stands whilst receiving a general overhaul in 1982.

Colin J. Marsden

A general view of the Lifting and Erecting Shop showing four Mk III coaches under construction. During most of the building period the main parts of the shell are held together in jigs. In the foreground a welder is seen putting the finishing touches to a roof section.

Litchurch Lane was engaged on a massive construction programme from the mid-1960s, building more than a thousand coaches of the Mk II design. The body shell of an FK vehicle is seen in this illustration with welders at work, busy on the later stages of assembly.

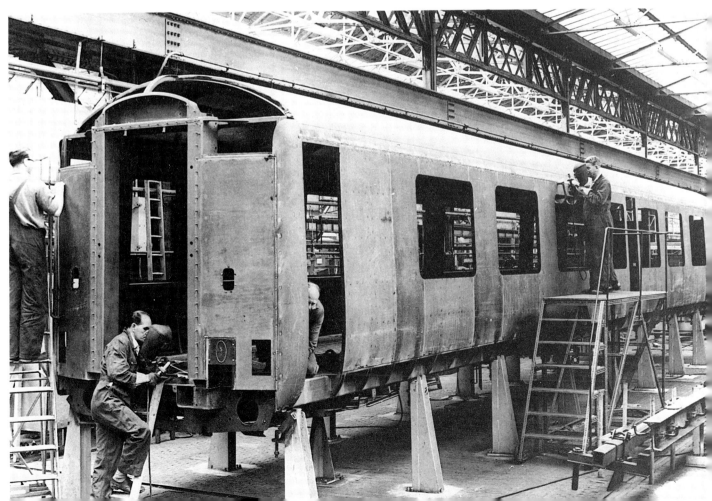

In 1981-82 no fewer than 208 Mk III sleeping vehicles were built by the Works, thus replacing the entire fleet of Mk I vehicles, dating back to the 1950s. Two different types of Mk III sleeper were produced, the SLEP, being a sleeper with pantry, and the SLE type which was of the same body design but without a pantry. A near-complete vehicle is lowered onto its bogies in this illustration of 2nd April 1982.

Colin J. Marsden

In common with all Mk IIIs constructed, the sleeping stock was of an all-steel, welded structure, this being of tremendous strength whilst still comparatively light weight, while meeting all the latest safety requirements in the field of fire/smoke penetration. Here wooden floor panels are seen being fitted.

BREL

After coach building was completed the 'empty' shell was transferred to the fitting out department, where side interior walls, ceilings, luggage racks and most important of all, the seats were installed. A fitter is seen screwing a seat to the floor whilst his colleague inspects an already fitted seat inside this Mk II vehicle.

Author's Collection

When vehicles were mechanically and internally complete the next stage was to finish the body work. After assembly the body was de-greased, primed, undercoated and finally given a top coat of gloss paint. Wearing the specified protective clothing a painter sprays the rail blue paint onto the side of a Mk II.

BREL

When the Advanced Passenger Train Prototype (APT-P) project was authorised, Litchurch Lane Works was awarded the construction contract for all but the power cars. The basic body shell of an APT Trailer Brake First (TBF) is seen taking shape.

BREL

In 1974 Litchurch Lane was awarded a contract to produce 20 Class 80 demus for Northern Ireland Railways (NIR). Part of this contract consisted of 20 Driving Trailer standard class coaches, one of which is seen under body assembly from the driving end. When introduced these units were numbered in the series 731-751.

Colin J. Marsden

As part of the Class 317 contract awarded to BREL, Litchurch Lane was given the responsibility to produce all intermediate trailer vehicles, the coaches then being transferred (between match wagons) to BREL York, where the remainder of the stock was constructed. One of the TS cars is seen receiving final testing before despatch to York.

Colin J. Marsden

BR ordered two prototype demus from BREL in 1981; one 3-car set and one 4-car set, both of which were constructed at Litchurch Lane. The 3-vehicle set No. 210002 is seen posed in the Work's yard whilst electrical testing was in progress. The DTS vehicle is nearest the camera.

Colin J. Marsden

One of the best known Litchurch Lane products of recent years has been various Railbus style vehicles which in all cases have been primarily formed of marrying a bus body to a rail chassis. The prototype Railbus R3 (RDB 977020) in its distinctive white, green and orange livery is seen in the Works' yard bearing both BRE and Leyland legends. This vehicle was later sold after testing on BR, to Northern Ireland Railways (NIR).

The successful Mk III coach body design has been utilized in the BREL export drive thus bringing considerable additional revenue to the Company. The Irish CIE network ordered 124 Mk III style vehicles which were delivered in 1983-84. The basic difference between these and the BR style is in the end doors, which on the CIE build were of the plug type. The first vehicle of the build is illustrated at the handing-over ceremony.

Colin J. Marsden

A large export order was won by BREL in 1980 for a fleet of passenger vehicles for the Tanzanian Railway. The stock loosely based on the BR Mk II design but by BR standards incorporated rather large windows and old fashioned corridor connections. A line of restaurant vehicles pose in Litchurch Lane yard mounted on 'ferry' bogies awaiting transfer to the docks for shipment.

After arrival from Leyland Bus, Workington, the bodies of Railbus vehicles were normally mounted on wagon chassis for movement around the works. This view shows various Class 141 bodies awaiting mounting on their correct wheelsets in December 1983.

Colin J. Marsden

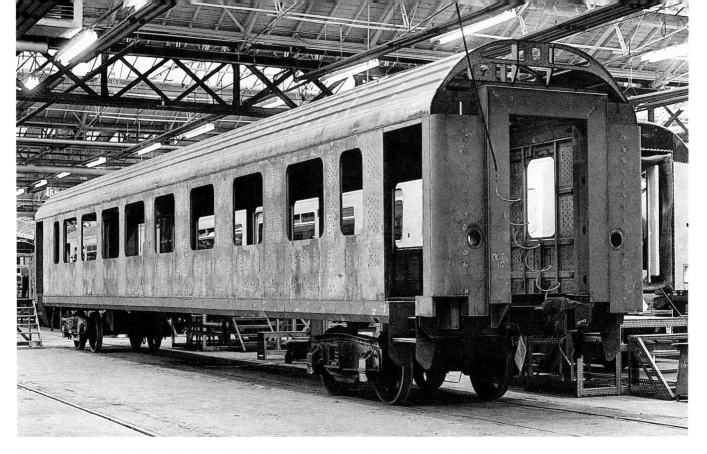

After BREL produced the International coach during the early 1980s as a shop window for the BREL export market, a substantial order was won from Gabon. One of the vehicles for this undertaking is seen in the Main Erecting Shop in October 1985 prior to any fitting out. Resemblance between this and the BR Mk III type is quite apparent.

Colin J. Marsden

During 1985 a substantial order for Class 451 dmu sets was awarded to BREL by Northern Ireland Railways. Body shell production was carried out at BREL York Works and detail finishing at Derby Litchurch Lane, the bodies being transported between the two Works by road. Two shells are seen mounted on accommodation underframes in the Litchurch Lane yard in company with a refurbished BR overhead line maintenance vehicle.

Colin J. Marsden

The private sector built Railbus bodies were almost 95% complete when arriving at Litchurch Lane, and if works' accommodation was available the road vehicle arriving with the body was taken directly into the Erecting Shop, where the body was removed for installation on its rail wheels. The upper photograph shows a Class 142 body on the rear of a telescopic articulated low-loader after arrival from Workington, while the lower illustration shows the same body only two hours later being married up with its rail wheels.

Both: Colin J. Marsden

The NIR Class 451 vehicles, after arrival from York took some four months to complete. The first of the build of driving vehicles is seen here just a few days before final body completion, mounted on four Matterson jacks. The close resemblance between this build and the BR Class 150 series is most obvious.

Colin J. Marsden

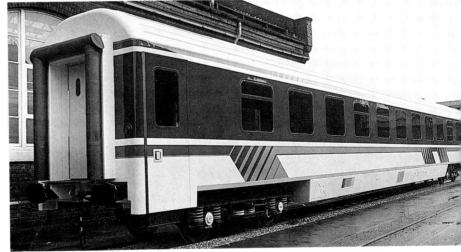

When the International coach was built as a demonstrator for possible overseas sales, considerable expense was placed on the vehicle. However due to the vehicle being assembled to the International loading gauge it was not permitted to leave the confines of Derby Litchurch Lane Works by rail. The vehicle is illustrated posed in the yard soon after completion.

In 1987-88 Mk III coach refurbishment was a major operation at the Works, resulting in vehicles being completely refitted internally, utilizing the latest methods of decor. Externally the coaches were finished in the new InterCity colours and sporting the latest Swallow motif and block *INTERCITY* lettering. A rake of four Mk IIIA FOs pose in the Litchurch Lane yard on 18th December 1987.

Brian Morrison

To provide traction units for the electrification of the Bournemouth-Weymouth line which opened in May 1988, a fleet of 24 5-car "Wessex Electric" Class 442 units worth some £30 million were constructed at Litchurch Lane. In this view a Motor Brake. Luggage Standard (MBLS) is seen under construction.

Brian Morrison

Driving Trailer Standard No. 77412 of "Wessex Electric" set No. 2407 takes shape in the main Erecting Shop at Litchurch Lane in December 1987. It will be seen that although the driver's front windows are of the wrap round type, a centre post is still provided, visible in the near cab window.

Brian Morrison

The first of the "Wessex Electric" sets was handed over to Network SouthEast Director, Mr Chris Green, in a ceremony at Derby on 18th December 1987. The very distinctive appearance of this new stock will surely make it some of the most impressive ever to operate on the SR. Driving Trailer Composite (DTC) of unit No. 2401 stands in the Works' yard.

Brian Morrison

Several traversers exist within the Litchurch Lane complex, each traverser bed being powered by a Litchurch Lane built overhead electric locomotive. During 1985 the illustrated propulsion unit, No. 4 was constructed to replace an old 1920s-built system.

Colin J. Marsden

Derby Locomotive

The second BREL establishment in Derby was the Locomotive Works, situated on the eastern side of the line adjacent to the City Station. The site of the Works was first acquired by the Midland Railway Company (MR) in 1840 and a small works constructed for the repair of the Company's railborne stock. The original 8 1/2 acre site expanded rapidly and by 1876 the MR had acquired a further site for the Carriage and Wagon business, leaving the original complex solely for the building, maintenance and repair of locomotives and allied products.

After the separation of the ways the Locomotive Works grew until it occupied a site of 51 acres. Derby Locomotive Works remained under the control of the Midland Railway until 1923, from when it was amalgamated into the London Midland & Scottish Railway Company (LMS), thus giving this Company two major locomotive factories, one at Derby and the other in Crewe. Under the 1948 railway nationalisation scheme, Derby Works was placed under the control of the BTC – Workshops Division, still having the same brief for locomotive manufacture and repair.

Official works' records show that the first steam locomotive was actually produced at the Works in mid-1851, from then until steam construction ceased in 1957 a total of 2,937 locomotives had been built.

Association of Derby Locomotive Works with modern traction, dates back to 1934, when an 0-6-0 steam chassis of 1891 vintage was rebuilt with new bodywork and a diesel power unit, to form 0-6-0 diesel shunter No. 1831. After the trials with diesel shunting traction, which proved totally successful, many subsequent orders were placed, but with outside contractors, or other works, Derby's share being quite small.

Modern traction construction until Nationalisation

Number Range	Type	Total	Years
1831	0-6-0	1	1934
7080-7119	0-6-0	40	1939-42
7120-7129	0-6-0	10	1945-47
10000	Co-Co	1	1947

In the twelve months leading up to railway nationalisation the LMS were keen to build main line diesel locomotives, and indeed the first main line diesel in the country, No. 10000, emerged late in 1947. In the immediate period following Nationalisation in January 1948, Derby continued with diesel building and received various shunter contracts and the construction order for the 'Fell' locomotive in 1951. With publication of the 1955 Modernisation Plan, which called for the full introduction of diesel and electric traction, Derby Works, with its past diesel history, was of course associated with this major step forward in rail history.

Details of Derby Locomotive Works construction to the Modernisation Plan are given below. Types indicated * were not constructed as a direct result of the modernisation scheme but are included to complete the Derby construction history. Apart form undertaking the construction of diesel locomotives the Works did, for many years, continue its association with steam traction fulfilling maintenance contracts.

Derby construction 1948-79:

Number Range	Type	Total	Years
10001*	Co-Co	1	1948
10100*	4-8-4	1	1951
12043-12102*	0-6-0	60	1948-52
D1-D10	1Co-Co1	10	1959-60
D11-D49	1Co-Co1	39	1960-61
D138-D193	1Co-Co1	56	1961-63
D3000-D3059	0-6-0	60	1952-54
D3082-D3126	0-6-0	45	1954-57
D3167-D3216	0-6-0	50	1955-56
D3245-D3297	0-6-0	53	1956-57
D3337-D3418	0-6-0	82	1957-58
D3503-D3571	0-6-0	69	1958
D3763-D3802	0-6-0	40	1959
D3937-D4010	0-6-0	74	1960
D5000-D5029	Bo-Bo	30	1958-59
D5066-D5075	Bo-Bo	10	1959-60
D5114-D5150	Bo-Bo	37	1960-61
D5186-D5222*	Bo-Bo	37	1963
D5233-D5299*	Bo-Bo	67	1963-65
D7500-D7577*	Bo-Bo	78	1964-65
D7598-D7623*	Bo-Bo	26	1966
D7660-D7677*	Bo-Bo	18	1966-67
49001-49006*	Bo-Bo+	6	1979

+ APT electric multiple unit power cars.

By 1965 the 'New Build' programmes were gradually run down, the Works then taking on the role of a major maintenance and repair facility for the large number of new generation classes. This activity remained at BREL Derby Locomotive Works but was much depleted in more recent years. Between 1960 and 1970 the Works was the major shunter overhaul point, as well as taking responsibility for Classes 20, 24, 25, 40, 44, 45 and 46 main line classes.

Following considerable rationalisation of the BR motive power fleet during the 1970s, alterations within the BREL structure, and the introduction of IC125s, Derby's workload was again amended with the Class 08 operation being transferred to Swindon. The Class 24s, which were coming up for retirement, together with the Class 40s moving to Crewe, left Derby with only a handful of Class 20, 25, the 'Peaks', and IC125 power cars to overhaul.

By the late-1980s, following complete withdrawal of Classes 24, 25, 44, 45 and 46 the main workload at Derby was the classified attention to IC125s, together with an ever decreasing number of Class 08 and 20. This work also came to an end in 1988 with no further scheduled overhauls due on Class 08 and 20 locomotives, while IC125 traction overhauls were transferred to regional Level 5 depots.

In 1973, when the Advanced Passenger Train – Experimental (APT-E), was under development at the Railway Technical Centre, the set spent several months at the Works whilst modifications were carried out, as well as being kept out of the public eye during a manning disagreement. The Work's association with the APT project continued in 1977-79 when the six electric power cars for the production sets were constructed, the vehicles subsequently returning to the Works on numerous occasions for modification and attention. Regrettably after the APT project was abandoned in 1986-87, the majority of cars were dismantled in the city of their birth.

Apart from construction and maintenance of locomotives and power cars, Derby Locomotive Works had the responsibility for the manufacture of bogies for all traction types, as well as dmu traction equipment repairs, power unit repairs and the overhaul of Mechnical & Electrical Engineers Department breakdown cranes for all regions of the railway.

A considerable number of withdrawn main line locomotives have been scrapped at Derby Works over the years. This operation ceasing in more recent times due to blue asbestos content in some locomotives which the Works could not deal with.

As well as carrying out work for the British market, Derby Locomotive Works effected a number of contracts to supply components to foreign railway administrations.

Upon privatisation Derby Locomotive Works concentrated on the supply of bogies and component parts – with no activity involving locomotives at all.

In 1988 the following main shops existed at Derby Locomotive Works:

In 1987 the following main shops existed at Derby Locomotive Works:

Crane Repair Shop This Shop occupied part of the original 1840 buildings (Roundhouse), being responsible for the overhaul and testing of most railway cranes and lifting tackle. Adjacent to the Shop was that of the Millwrights, catering for the maintenance and installation of plant and machinery within the works.

Traction Motor Repair Shop Here the maintenance and testing of traction motors and associated equipment was undertaken, both overhead and underfloor conveyor systems were provided.

Wheel Shop All wheel work was undertaken within this Shop – with maintenance of existing sets and the fabrication of new wheels, bogies and axles.

Fabrication Shop This consisted of seven bays and work carried out included the manufacture of new bogie frames and the forming of parts to repair locomotive damage. Shop facilities including large presses and furnaces for forming components, boom welding units, large multi-head flame cutters, milling and drilling machines.

Boiler, Cab & Tank Repair Shop Steam heating boilers (until 1984), heat exchangers, radiators, tanks, reservoirs, locomotive cabs, fixtures and fittings were repaired or modified in this Shop.

Electric Shop A major part of this Shop was devoted to the rebuilding of locomotive main generators and repairs to traction motor armatures, in addition to much miscellaneous electrical work.

Pump Room This purpose-built 'clean room' contained special devices to ensure cleanliness during the overhaul of fuel pumps, fuel injectors and governors, special calibration equipment being provided.

Generator Shop Main generator castings, brush gear and armatures were dealt with in this area. Special facilities existed to ensure clean and dry working conditions.

Locomotive Bogie Repair Shop All locomotive bogies were stripped, cleaned (in a high pressure washing plant) and reassembled here. Special bogie traversers were provided to assist with movement.

Diesel Repair Shop All locomotives requiring attention visited this Shop where they were lifted clear of their bogies, components removed and sent for repair. Body repairs were then carried out and reassembly work commenced.

Bogie Assembly Shop Adjacent to the Diesel Repair Shop was the Bogie assembly area dealing with the manufacture of new locomotive, carriage, and wagon bogies for all BREL Workshops and some European administrations.

Fitting Shop This Shop was responsible for the repair and overhaul of locomotive components including power units, auxiliary equipment and brake units. A special cleaning plant was provided.

Machine Shop The usual array of modern specialised computer controlled metalworking machines were found in this area, dealing with most 'on works' requirements.

Railcar Engine Shop Although Derby Locomotive did not deal with dmu vehicles it operated a large department solely for heavy maintenance to railcar engines, with adjacent purpose-constructed test bays.

Heavy Machine Shop This housed the larger engineering machines being principally engaged on the machining of bogie components.

Test House/Area To ensure that all locomotives and power cars outshopped by the Works met the necessary performance standards, special locomotive and IC125 test facilities were provided.

Paint Shop Before returning to traffic after receiving classified attention most vehicles passed through this area for cosmetic attention.

Apart from the Shops mentioned above the Works contained other smaller work units including a De-fuelling Apron, Joinery & Plastics Shop, Sheet Metal Shop, Spring Shop and Blacksmiths' Plant.

In addition to the work's main activity buildings a full support section was provided. This included a large Training School, several Stores, a Staff Canteen, a Medical Centre, and a sizeable office complex.

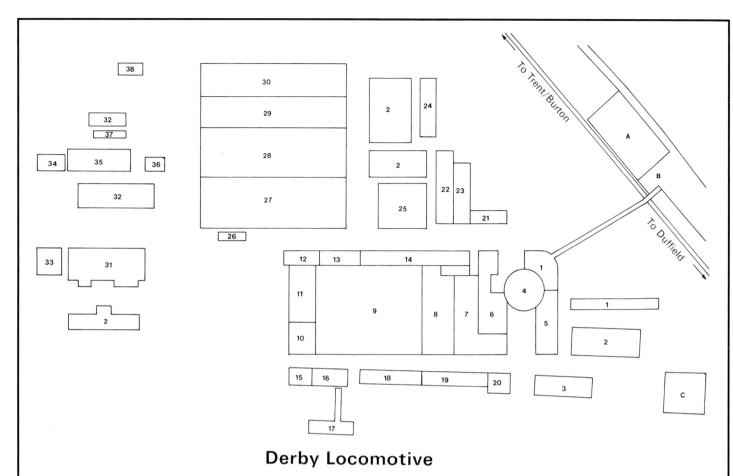

Derby Locomotive

A   Derby Station
B   Footbridge to Works
C   Main Works Entrance

1   Works Offices
2   Stores
3   Works Canteen
4   Crane Repair Shop

5   Works Millwright Shop
6   Works Training School
7   Traction Motor and Auxiliary Machine Repair Shop
8   Wheel Shop
9   Main Fabrication Shop
10 Steam Generator Repair Shop
11 Locomotive Reservoir and Cab Repair Shop

12 Generator Repair Shop
13 Electrical Cubicle Repair Shop
14 Electrical Equipment Repair Shop
15 Metal Plate Preparation Plant
16 Materials Spray Painting Shop
17 Works Power Station
18 Sheet Metal Shop
19 Smiths' Shop
20 Spring Repair/Manufacture Shop
21 Training Centre
22 Generator 'Clean Room' Shop
23 Pump 'Clean Room' Repair Shop
24 Joinery and Plastics Shop
25 Locomotive Bogie Cleaning/Repair Shop
26 Defuelling Apron
27 Diesel Locomotive/IC125 Repair Shop
28 Fitting Shop
29 Machine Shop
30 New Bogie and Wheel Shop
31 DMU Engine Repair Shop
32 Paint Shop
33 DMU Engine Test House
34 HST Power Car Test Area
35 Heavy Machine Shop
36 HST Engine Test House
37 Gearbox Repair Shop
38 Locomotive Test House

This is the first view that the public see of Derby Locomotive Works when arriving at the City station. The building latterly used for the repair of cranes, together with some office accommodation above, forms part of the original Works building. On top of this is the famous Derby Works Clock Tower with a beautiful weathervane, cast in the shape of a Midland Railway locomotive.

Colin J. Marsden

Derby was the first workshop in the country to undertake diesel locomotive assembly. In this view, taken in 1947 with the Works still under the control of the LMS, six 0-6-0 diesel shunters are seen under construction. On the right of the Shop a number of power units are seen being assembled.

Author's Collection

Following the 1955 Modernisation Plan Derby Locomotive Works was granted construction contracts for a number of Type 2 and Type 4 locomotives. In this view one of the first Type 2 locomotives, later of Class 24, is seen under test on the Locomotive Test Centre.

Author's Collection

Throughout the early 1960s the Erecting Shop at Derby contained an almost continual stream of Type 2 locomotives with a total of 303 being built at the Works. Five of the later body styled Type 2s forming Class 25 are seen under assembly in 1963.
Author's Collection

The Derby Works Roundhouse. The last remaining polygonal timber roofed structure in the country was used in recent years for the repair of cranes, the turntable in the centre of this view being retained in an operational state. This building is of course listed and cannot be demolished.
J. Harris

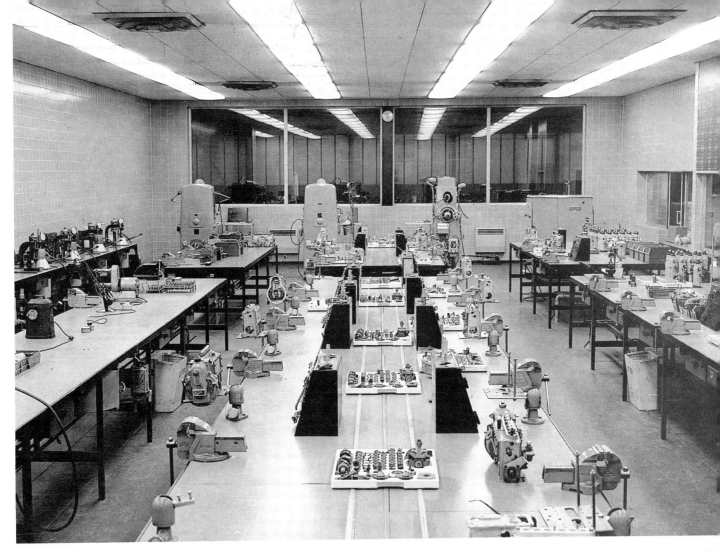

To ensure cleanliness of such costly items as fuel pumps, fuel injectors and engine governors, a special 'clean room' was provided. The walls were specially tiled and doors air-sealed, all ensuring a spotless working condition. This view shows the Shop with test equipment at the far end.

An outstation to the main Works complex was the Railcar Engine Repair Shop illustrated with adjoining test facility. This Shop dealt with the progressive repair of dmu power units, not only for BREL use but for regional depot requirements.

A sizeable Bogie Construction & Repair Department was provided in the main Works complex. An IC125 power bogie receives a final coat of paint before being transferred to the Repair Shop for installation under an overhauled vehicle.
Colin J. Marsden

Coupled to the drive flange of all diesel electric power units is a generator/alternator, providing electric current for the traction motors which in turn rotate the road wheels. The generators have a special Shop within the Works for their overhaul. Here a generator armature is seen being lowered into a cleaning bath.

With BREL's ever increasing interest in the export field, some of the Group's undertakings in latter years carried out work for foreign administrations, Derby Locomotive Works Bogie Shop usually being used to supply bogies or wheelsets. This illustration shows a 3ft 6in gauge bogie built for Taiwan mounted on temporary narrow gauge track prior to packing and despatch.

In 1974-75 withdrawn Class 08 Nos D3047, D3092, D3098, and D3100 were sold to Lamco, a Liberian mining company which operated a railway network. As part of the contract the machines were given a classified overhaul at Derby prior to export, being repainted in Lamco orange and cream livery.

Colin J. Marsden

During the late 1970s a considerable quantity of man hours and vast expenditure was placed on the Advanced Passenger Train (APT) project, with one complete Shop at Derby Locomotive Works set aside for the construction of the six powered vehicles. In this view one car is seen nearing body completion, while another on the far left is in an early stage of assembly.

The sight of a row of 'Peaks' in Derby Works is now a thing of the past with all casual and classified overhauls long since finished. In this view, taken on 30th September 1985, Class 45/0 Nos 45012 and 45051 stand in the main Repair Shop while intermediate overhauls are carried out.
Colin J. Marsden

When numbers of main line locomotives visited the works their cabs were often removed for attention, especially if panels were damaged or corroded. Here a fitter selects an item from his toolbox whilst working on a Class 25 cab. Parts of a 'Peak' cab can be seen in the background.
Colin J. Marsden

The main activity at the Locomotive Repair Shop in recent years was the maintenance and overhaul of IC125 power cars. This general view of the Shop taken in 1981, shows three power cars and four 'Peaks' under repair. Note the general cleanliness of the working area – an important factor for an efficient and safe workshop.

In the early 1980s some Class 20 classified overhauls were undertaken by Derby, Crewe and Glasgow Works. These overhauls were effected as it was projected that these Type 1 locomotives would remain in service for several years, and in a number of instances their overhaul included fitting of dual brake equipment. Our view here shows No. 20108 awaiting final completion at Derby on 30th September 1985.

Colin J. Marsden

Although scheduled for only 18 months additional work, in 1985 a number of Class 45/1 locomotives were still to be found receiving classified attention at the Works. This view shows No. 45115 mounted in special 'Peak' slings on the shop floor whilst an intermediate overhaul was effected.

Colin J. Marsden

With the astonishingly high mileage achieved by the IC125 fleet their visits to the Works for classified attention was quite frequent. WR allocated DMB No. 43055 is shown during a general overhaul in September 1985. When the power car was released to traffic the redundant guard's accommodation was removed and the latest InterCity livery applied.

Colin J. Marsden

When IC125 power cars received attention at Derby it was usual to find about ten on works at the same time. The duration of works overhaul being dependent upon the level of repair and condition of components, but on average cars were at works for around four weeks. No. 43047 *Rotherham Enterprise* is illustrated.

Colin J. Marsden

After crane repairs were carried out a thorough test programme was always performed, because a failure of one of these essential pieces of equipment could have tragic consequences. In this view diesel hydraulic crane No. ADRC96717, originally built as a steam crane in 1939, stands in the Works yard during lifting trials. In latter years this crane, with a lifting capacity of 45 tons has been allocated to Inverness.

Colin J. Marsden

Doncaster

The BREL undertaking at Doncaster had its origins as far back as 1853 when the Great Northern Railway Company (GNR) purchased an 11 acre site on the west side of the line, adjacent to the town's station. The original works consisted of ten small shops with a covered area of just 4½ acres. This should be compared with the undertaking in 1985 which occupied over 84 acres, 50% of which was covered accommodation.

During the later years of the 19th century the works – known locally as 'The Plant' – produced many hundreds of steam locomotives, carriages and wagon stock. As production increased the premises gradually expanded and further larger shops were erected.

In 1923 the Works came under the control of the London & North Eastern Railway Company (LNER) who subsequently favoured the Works with a number of building and maintenance contracts. Over the years the Works was responsible for the production of some splendid and world famous steam locomotives, such as the Stirling 8ft Singles, Ivatt Atlantics, *Flying Scotsman*, and the world steam speed record holder *Mallard*. In common with all other works Doncaster came under the control of the BTC Workshops Division from January 1948 and formed a major undertaking within the BREL Company after its formation in January 1970.

Doncaster's association with modern traction can be traced back to 1941, when 1,500v dc electric locomotive No. 6000 was constructed. This locomotive later became LNER No. 6701 and BR No. E26000 *Tommy* – being the forerunner to the Manchester-Sheffield-Wath Class 76 fleet. Diesel traction building commenced during 1944 with the first of four 0-6-0 diesel prototypes. Modern traction building continuing right to the end of BREL's reign at Doncaster in 1987.

Doncaster modern traction building programme:

Type	Class	Total	Years
–	(76)	1	1941
–	*	4	1944-45
–	**	1	1949
–	03	82	1958-61
–	08	30	1957-59
4	71	24	1959-60
4	85	40	1961-63
4	86	40	1965-66
5	56	85	1977-83
5	58	50	1983-87

*Four experimental/prototype 0-6-0 shunters.
**One Brush/BR prototype 0-6-0 shunter.

From the mid-1960s alterations within the Workshop Division gave Doncaster one of the Group's major roles, with the emphasis being placed on maintenance and repair work. In addition to locomotives it also covered dmus, coaching and wagon stock. In more recent years the Works was responsible for the major construction programme of both the Class 56 and 58 fleets, as well as the building of wagons for BR, British private operations and foreign administrations. The Works was also responsible for production of eleven battery electric locomotives for the London Transport Executive in 1974.

Probably the most important event at Doncaster Works during the BREL administration was the Class 56 'New Build' contract, which commenced in 1975, with the first locomotive No. 56031 being completed in just two years. Various follow up contracts for Class 56s were placed with the Works, leading to a Doncaster production run of 85 examples. However, difficulties within the Works and the supply industries in general gave a protracted delivery period with on average only one locomotive emerging per month.

During 1982-83 it was decided to commence construction of the next generation of freight locomotive – the Class 58 – at Doncaster Works, thus giving a continued 'New Build' programme until 1987. The pleasure of the Class 58 contract was marred slightly by a Board decision to transfer construction of the final 20 Class 56s to BREL Crewe Works. This transfer gave an even longer production timescale for an already late running class. A major Works' achievement worthy of note in more recent years was the total refurbishment of the Class 50 fleet, providing the Works with a five year contract.

Under major BREL rationalisation of the mid-1980s Doncaster Works was closed with effect from mid-1987, the locomotive and unit repair facility being handed over to BRML as a major Level 5 depot, while the redundant dmu repair building became a new multi-million pound 'Railpart' National Stores Centre, operated by the Director of Mechanical Engineering. The Wagon Works remained under BREL control until Autumn 1987 when it was offered for sale to the private sector – the eventual purchasers being RFS Industries, incorporating a group of former senior Works management. This facility now continues in the wagon construction and maintenance field, as well as effecting general maintenance operations on BR rolling stock, including replacement transmissions on a number of 'Pacer' and 'Skipper' units, and the classified overhauls to diesel locomotives. This work has been awarded on a competitive tender basis. During 1987, when the changeover of ownership of Doncaster Wagon Works was underway, a major contract for producing BR China Clay hoppers was being fulfilled, these being a direct descendant of the time-honoured mgr wagon, and used for ECC traffic.

Under the BRML arrangements the new Level 5 depot is responsible for classified attention to many main line classes, as well as some conventional dmu vehicles and new generation diesel stock.

A guide to the main Shops of Doncaster Works towards the end of BREL days is given:

Dismantling Shop Upon arrival at the Works, the first work on locomotives after de-fuelling was stripping. Locomotives being lifted clear of their bogies, steam cleaned, and all major components removed to various other Shops within the Works for attention. From the Dismantling Shop locomotives were usually placed on accommodation bogies and taken to the Main Repair Shop.

Diesel Locomotive Repair Shop This housed the main hub of Works activity having a floor area of 140,000 sq ft, devoted to the building of new locomotives, repairing existing fleets and the rebuilding of power units and bogies. The main Repair Shop, divided into three sections: 2-bay,

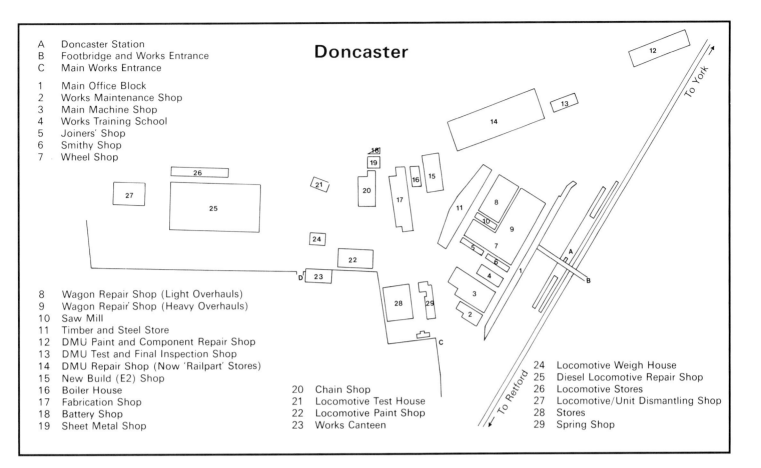

Doncaster

A Doncaster Station
B Footbridge and Works Entrance
C Main Works Entrance

1 Main Office Block
2 Works Maintenance Shop
3 Main Machine Shop
4 Works Training School
5 Joiners' Shop
6 Smithy Shop
7 Wheel Shop

8 Wagon Repair Shop (Light Overhauls)
9 Wagon Repair Shop (Heavy Overhauls)
10 Saw Mill
11 Timber and Steel Store
12 DMU Paint and Component Repair Shop
13 DMU Test and Final Inspection Shop
14 DMU Repair Shop (Now 'Railpart' Stores)
15 New Build (E2) Shop
16 Boiler House
17 Fabrication Shop
18 Battery Shop
19 Sheet Metal Shop
20 Chain Shop
21 Locomotive Test House
22 Locomotive Paint Shop
23 Works Canteen
24 Locomotive Weigh House
25 Diesel Locomotive Repair Shop
26 Locomotive Stores
27 Locomotive/Unit Dismantling Shop
28 Stores
29 Spring Shop

3-bay and 4-bay, having high capacity overhead cranes enabling complete locomotives to be lifted if required. At the west end of the Shop was a Wheelbay, while adjacent to the Diesel Locomotive Repair Shop was a sizeable Diesel Store. After closure of the dmu shop for rebuilding as the new Central Stores, a number of unit vehicles were overhauled in this Shop.

Diesel Test House A state of the art, purpose-built Test House, capable of housing two locomotives at one time was provided, being used to test new machines and repaired locomotives prior to active testing. A test apron was also provided with sound-insulated walls.

Chain Shop This Shop undertook repairs and testing of chains and other lifting tackle, being equipped with a 100 ton capacity test rig. For a number of years part of this Shop was used to manufacture agricultural equipment for the private sector.

Locomotive Paint Shop A large Paint Shop. Adjacent to the Kirk Street entrance was provided, where all locomotives and some NPCCS vehicles were taken for detail completion. A test booth for flash testing of new products was also housed here. The Shop was also responsible for painting many small component parts, and works equipment.

Fabrication Shop This Shop had two main bays, one dealing with plate preparation including oxy-cutting and sub-assembly work, whilst the other carried out assembly operations. Adjoining the Fabrication Shop was the Flanging Shop equipped with a 100 ton and 750 ton presses.

New Build Shop Known within the Works as 'E2' Shop, this was where most new assembly work was undertaken, including all the Doncaster Class 56s, 20 Class 58s and a number of wagons.

Diesel Multiple Unit Repair Shop This sizeable building looked after all dmmu stock. Upon arrival, cars were lifted from their bogies and progressed along a repair line. Whilst bodies were worked on, bogies were passed to the Bogie Shop for overhaul. Full facilities existed for mechanical and electrical repairs, whilst another section was devoted to re-assembly and vehicle finishing. At the north end of the Shop was a dmu Test House. In 1986 this Shop was closed, gutted and rebuilt as the new DM&EE 'Railpart' Central Stores, coming on stream progressively from Spring 1987.

Machine Shop This department carried out machining and fitting of components for repaired stock. A number of modern computer controlled machines were used.

Wagon Repair Shop Two sizeable Wagon Repair Plants were situated towards the north end of the Works complex, one dealing with heavy overhauls and assembly work, and the other light maintenance. The Heavy Shop effected work on high capacity coal wagons, brakevans, covered goods wagons, open vehicles as well as assembly of new products. The Shop was divided into three main bays, traversers were installed to assist in wagon movement and special sections provided for wheel, axle and axlebox repair. The Light Shop was responsible for general wagon repairs utilizing the flowline principle again a traverser was fitted as were overhead cranes. Following the demise of the BREL operation this section was sold to RFS Industries.

Following the mass withdrawal of a number of diesel classes including 03, 08, 13, 24, 25, 40, 45, 46 and 55 the Works was, for a number of years, under contract to BR to dismantle obsolete locomotives and reclaim any suitable components for re-use.

Adjacent to Doncaster Railway Station, was the BREL main Office Complex incorporating a sumptuous Work's Manager's suite – the same one once used by Sir Nigel Gresley. A sizeable Works Training School and Canteen were also provided, together with a full Medical Centre and ample provision for social activities.

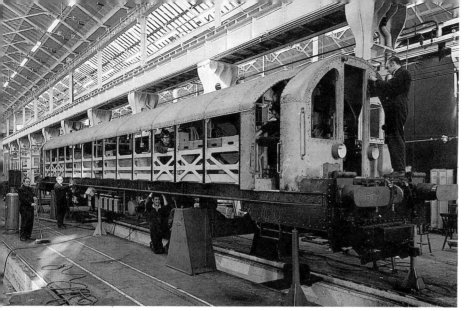

As part of BREL's services to outside industry a fleet of eleven battery electric locomotives were constructed at Doncaster for London Transport's Civil Engineering Section in 1973-74. A nearly completed example is illustrated at the final body assembly stage in November 1973.

Colin J. Marsden

No fewer than 85 Class 56 freight locomotives were built by the Works between May 1979 and January 1983. This illustration shows the near completed body of No. 56035 being lowered onto its bogies with the aid of two 45 tonne gantry cranes in the Works E2 Shop.

Colin J. Marsden

Under the watchful eye of Works Management and Design Department staff, the first steel plate members for the pioneer Class 58 are seen being cut on a multi-head flame cutter in the Works Fabrication Shop. The items being prepared were the top and bottom plates of the main girder longitudinals.

Derek Porter

The first 20 Class 58s were assembled in the original New Build or E2 Shop, while the remainder were manufactured in the main Diesel Repair Shop. After the Class 58 underframes were completed they were placed on a manipulator and inverted, enabling fitting staff to assemble the underside. Two frames, that of No. 58010 on the left and No. 58009 (inverted) on the right, are seen in E2 Shop on 5th July 1983.

Colin J. Marsden

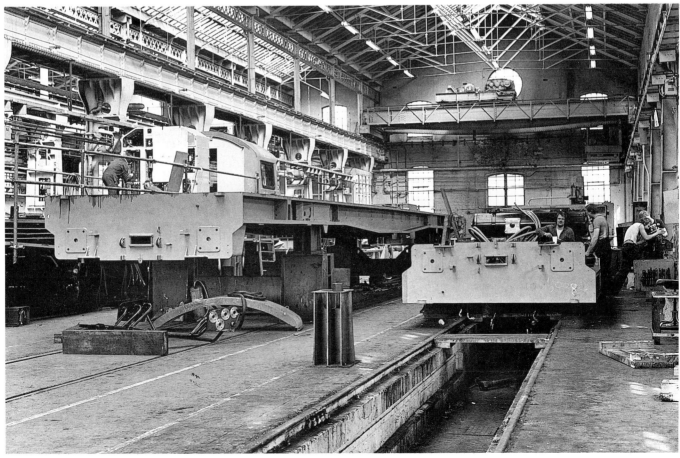

A completed cab module of a Class 58 stands on its back during final welding in the Fabrication Shop. When finished the cab would be taken to the Paint Shop and then internally fitted out prior to installation.

Colin J. Marsden

Surrounded by thousands of component parts that go to form a Class 58, No. 58026 with cab and cooler group intact, rests on accommodation stands in the Main Shop in November 1982. Depending on availability of components each Class 58 spent about three months on above floor construction.

Colin J. Marsden

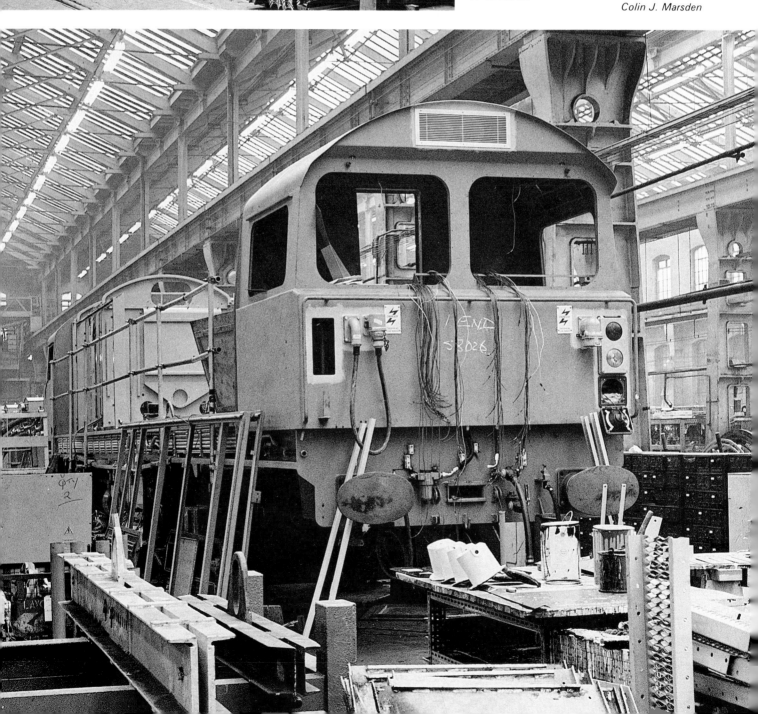

A contract to supply flat wagons to Gabon was won by BREL in 1984. The building work was given to Doncaster who carried out construction in the New Build Shop, the first completed vehicle emerging in December 1984, photographed in the Works yard.

Colin J. Marsden

Internal movement of locomotives within the Works always caused something of a problem. Usually main line locomotives were mounted on trolley or accommodation bogies, but when it came to shunters, Doncaster mounted the bodies on flat beds and hauled them round the plant with a road tractor. This method of transport is illustrated by Class 03 No. 03094.

John Tuffs

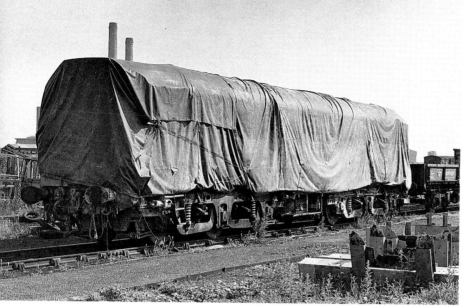

If locomotives suffered considerable damage due to fire or collision they were usually covered in tarpaulins for movement around the railway system, this not only kept the damage out of public view but protected the stock from further damage caused by adverse weather. Class 31 No. 31214 damaged in a collision at Hope in May 1983 is seen 'under wraps' in the Works yard.

Colin J. Marsden

After a break of some five years Doncaster resumed Class 08 overhauls in 1983, with mainly 'casual' repairs, however, from 1986 classified overhauls returned to Doncaster. No. 08540 is shown in No. 4 bay receiving crank arm repairs on 5th July 1983.

Colin J. Marsden

Since their introduction in the 1960s through until 1984 the majority of Class 37 classified overhauls were undertaken by Doncaster. Following altered works practices, Class 37 major overhauls including refurbishment, were transferred to BREL Crewe, leaving Doncaster with only a handful of casual overhauls. No. 37212 is pictured in No. 2 bay on 15th October 1981.

Colin J. Marsden

One of the major sources of employment for the locomotive repair staff between February 1978 and May 1983 was the complete refurbishment of the Class 50 fleet, bringing each example to the Plant for around five months. No. 50031 *Hood* is seen midway through its refurbishment in September 1981.

Colin J. Marsden

After spending many hours working on carriage washing duties, where acid was used in the water, a rather bleached Class 03 No. 03063 stands towards the rear of the Works No. 4 bay on 21st August 1981, after arrival at the Works for a classified overhaul. Special attention would have been given to the external cleaning of this locomotive prior to painting to ensure that all traces of corrosive had been removed.

Colin J. Marsden

Class 50 No. 50009 *Conqueror* and Class 37/0 No. 37244 pose side by side in the Main Erecting Shop during respective refurbishment/general overhauls. As can be seen, space was very restricted within the Main Shop.

Colin J. Marsden

Concurrent with the first Class 50 refurbishments the final intermeduate overhauls of the previous repair contract were still being completed. No. 50047 *Swiftsure* stands in 4-bay in late 1979 whilst undergoing an intermediate.

Colin J. Marsden

The only BREL Works in recent years to undertake Class 31 repairs was Doncaster, with machines normally receiving classified attention every four to five years. This picture shows No. 31217 receiving unscheduled repairs following heavy buffer impact. Note the jacks supporting the underside of the buffer beam whilst straightening is carried out.

Colin J. Marsden

This general view of the Works yard shows the area to the front of the main repair shop, with the 2-road test house in the centre background. Various members of Classes 31, 37 and 55 can be seen in the yard together with two Class 03s. The Class 37 in the foreground, No. 37199 is coupled to a Works' resistor unit used for locomotive output testing.

Colin J. Marsden

With its body weight supported by two 45-ton Heywood gantry cranes, Class 31/1 No. 31151 is lifted in the Stripping Shop for positioning on accommodation stands, whilst internal items are removed. When this locomotive emerged from works it was fitted with Electric Train Supply and renumbered 31436.

Colin J. Marsden

The Class 31/1 locomotives that received heavy general overhauls (HGO) at Doncaster during the 1980s, underwent major surgery with virtually all body panels being replaced. No. 31247 completely gutted, is seen in 3-bay on 12th February 1987.

Colin J. Marsden

A frequent BREL customer in later years was the National Railway Museum (NRM), York, who had a number of their exhibits repaired at various workshops. Doncaster was responsible for the repair and repainting to the nationally preserved Classes 20, 31, 55, 71 and 76 on the modern traction scene. Pioneer Class 20 No. D8000 disguised as No. 20050 stands in the Works yard awaiting attention on 5th July 1983. This machine was restored to its original green livery in Spring 1985.

Colin J. Marsden

A Doncaster masterpiece. After arrival in a decrepit condition painted in rail blue and carrying the number 31018, D5500 the original ''Toffee Apple'' Brush Type 2, stands at the Works in immaculate condition awaiting return to the NRM on 10th September 1977.

Colin J. Marsden

Another Doncaster Works activity for a number of years was the repair of Civil Engineering Department cranes, but by the mid-1980s this operation drew to a close. After receiving attention each crane was put through a stringent safety test which included periods of lifting weightblocks. This testing was normally carried out near the Paint Shop. ER crane No. DRF81144 is shown.

Colin J. Marsden

In latter years a major Doncaster activity was the dismantling of redundant locomotives. Depending on which parts, if any, were required for further use, the machines were stripped internally first, or gutted by the breaking up staff. Locomotives of Classes 03, 08, 13, 24, 25, 31, 40, 45, 46 and 55 were dismantled at the Works. The upper illustration shows Class 40 Nos 40199 and 40128 awaiting their call to the breaker's line, while the lower picture shows 'Deltic' No. 55010 (*The King's Own Scottish Borderer*) midway through breaking up.

Colin J. Marsden

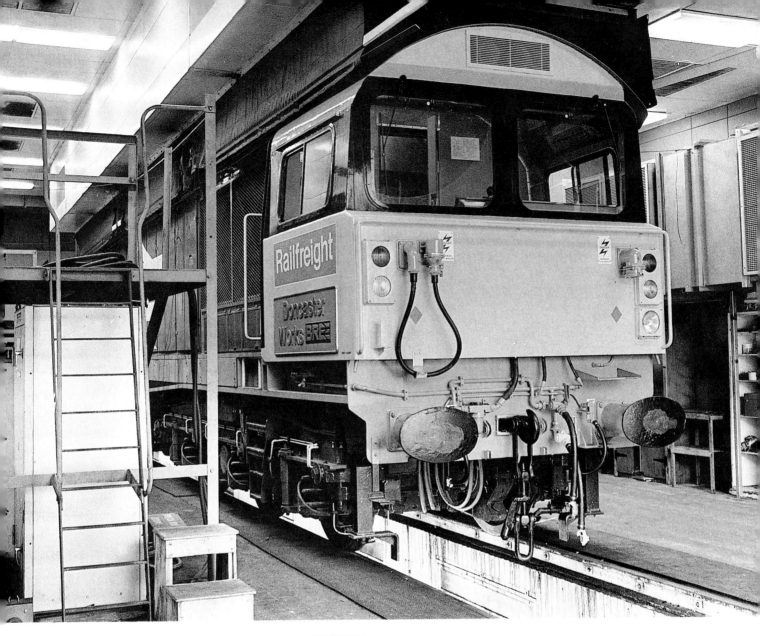

After completion of new or repaired locomotives a thorough testing period took place, which usually meant locomotives spending a day or so in the soundproofed Test House, where power units could be run up and the performance evaluated. Class 58 No. 58020 *Doncaster Works BRE* stands inside the Test House whilst being prepared for alternator output tests. This locomotive was later renamed *Doncaster Works*.

Colin J. Marsden

Usually, after the 'on works' test period, main line locomotives operated an active road test hauling a designated set of Departmental coaches between Doncaster and Newcastle or Peterborough. On 21st May 1982 the test train, headed by immaculate Class 37 No.37260 was photographed at Dalton-on-Tees, near Darlington.

Colin J. Marsden

To cater for the training of works apprentices, a fully equipped Training School was provided. This could accommodate some 80 craft trainees usually on a one year off the job programme. The main entrance of the Training School is illustrated.

Colin J. Marsden

Doncaster Wagon Repair Shop was also responsible for overhauls and maintenance to selected NPCCS stock. A newspaper packing van is seen receiving attention from the signwriters in this view, showing that not all bodyside legends were transfers.

The Works Central Wheel Shop repaired and produced wheels for locomotives, multiple units, loco-hauled coaches and freight vehicles. In this illustration a fitter is seen preparing a new tyre for turning, whilst two others await attention in the foreground.

A privately owned 'Presflo' powdered cement wagon is illustrated during an extensive refit operation in the New Build Shop. BREL establishments were available to tender for the overhaul of private sector stock and usually won a sizeable proportion of the market.

Some Mk I passenger vehicles received attention at Doncaster in the 1980s, usually in the Wagon Repair Shop. In this picture we see SK No. 25838 receiving an internal refit. Note the seats and seatbacks stacked up awaiting removal.

Colin J. Marsden

Supported on works accommodation stands, LMR Civil Engineers Observation Saloon No. DBM999504 allocated to Derby, poses in the Wagon Shop on 12th September 1981, during a classified overhaul. The 10 tonne Matterson screwjack in the foreground – one of four – would have been used in lifting the body off its bogies.

Colin J. Marsden

Class 110 DMC No. E52066 stands outside the Diesel Unit Test House. By the condition of its underframe equipment it is apparant that reconditioned bogies and engines have been installed, and these were undoubtedly awaiting testing prior to the vehicle's return to traffic.

Colin J. Marsden

The Diesel Multiple Unit Repair Shop had facilities to house 15-20 vehicles at any one time. Class 123 "Trans-Pennine" driving car No. E51951 receives its last repair on 12th September 1981 prior to withdrawal. Note that part of the car number is carried in the former route indicator box.

Colin J. Marsden

Staff safety was one of the most important factors in all Shops. Stores were carried on a trolley to avoid the lifting of heavy weights by staff and a special ladder is seen propped against the cab doorway of Class 101 DMBS No. E51221.

Colin J. Marsden

Class 114 DMBS No. E50037 awaits final testing in the DMU Test House. The notice hanging from the roof of the building informs staff that they must not start work on a vehicle until stipulated safety conditions are met.

Colin J. Marsden

In the closing months of BREL's reign at Doncaster a number of Class 31s were released painted in the new Railfreight grey livery, sporting a red solebar band. The second of the Doncaster red-banded Class 31s, No. 31180, poses inside No. 4 bay on 12th February 1987, alongside collision damaged sister No. 31405.

Colin J. Marsden

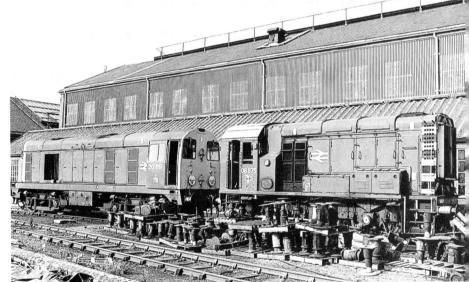

After BREL's handover of the Works to BRML, Class 20 and 47 locomotives started to receive attention at the complex. On 3rd October 1987 No. 20119, in company with Class 08 No. 08875, poses in the yard awaiting admittance to the Repair Shop.

Brian Morrison

To coincide with the official opening of the new BRML Plant at Doncaster, and the facilities recently acquired association with the Class 47 fleet, No. 47522 was outshopped in mock LNER green livery and named *Doncaster Enterprise*, at a special Open Day event on 3rd October 1987.

Brian Morrison

Eastleigh

British Rail Engineering, Eastleigh was the most southerly works within the Group, situated in Hampshire, close to the City of Southampton. The Works was positioned at the southern end of Eastleigh station on the eastern side of the line, adjacent to Eastleigh Diesel Depot. The complex now forms part of the BRML operation.

In years past, Eastleigh sported two railway workshops, one with responsibility for carriage and wagon stock, and the other locomotives. The carriage works was built in 1891 by the London & South Western Railway (LSWR) on a site to the north of the late BREL works, having responsibility for all carriage, wagon and container repairs, remaining in operation until 1968. At the time the LSWR opened Eastleigh Carriage & Wagon Works, locomotive building and heavy maintenance was undertaken at Nine Elms in South London. However, from 1909 a major policy change took place, when the LSWR purchased additional land to the south of the Carriage Works and Eastleigh Locomotive Works was constructed. Both of Eastleigh's works later came under the control of the Southern Railway Company, and operated alongside the Company's other workshops at Brighton, Ashford and Lancing.

The main activities at Eastleigh Carriage Works during the 1920-1940s were the construction of new coaches and containers and the repair of coaches, containers and wagons. A milestone in the Work's history came in 1945 when the first all-steel passenger coach was completed. In the years between 1923 and Nationalisation the Locomotive Works was employed in the building and repair of steam traction and anciliary equipment; modern locomotive operations coming to Eastleigh in the early 1960s. However, the Works was only responsible for the construction of one modern traction fleet as demonstrated below, but has always played a major role in locomotive and stock maintenance.

Eastleigh Works modern traction locomotive building:

Class	Total	Year
73/0	6	1962

In addition to the above, Eastleigh Works has been responsible for the construction of numerous SR emu and dmu vehicles, ranging from suburban to InterCity types.

From 1948 both works came under the control of the BTC, remaining in full operation in their dedicated fields. However, some responsibilities were altered in respect of changing maintenance needs, but the general position remained unchanged until 1962, when a major reorganisation of the BR workshops took place. These changes gave Eastleigh Locomotive Works the complete responsibility for the Region's motive power, thus taking over the work previously carried out at both Ashford and Brighton. At the same time the Works took over repair responsibilities for modern traction locomotives and units.

An interesting twist to Eastleigh's construction history came in 1961-62 when the six prototype electro-diesels (now Class 73/0) were constructed at the Carriage Works, a practice which was rather frowned upon by staff in the Locomotive Works.

Between 1964-68 further major reorganisation of Eastleigh Works took place. This included much-needed modernisation of most Shops within the Locomotive Works to cater for all repair needs of the future, and regrettably the complete closure of the original Carriage Works, whose previous repair responsibility was concentrated on the Locomotive Works. After reorganisation the complex was renamed just Eastleigh Works.

From January 1970 Eastleigh Works came under the BREL flag being responsible for classified overhauls to Southern Region main line locomotives, as well as selected (mainly SR) shunting locomotives, all SR emu/dmu fleets, plus some ER emu classes, as well as a wide variety of passenger, NPCCS and wagon stock. The acreage of the Works in 1970 was 41, of which eleven was covered buildings. In 1982 there were some 2,500 staff employed, a greatly reduced figure to that of the past.

With the introduction of the new manufacture and maintenance policy of the BRB in 1987, and the formation of the British Rail Maintenance Ltd, BREL Eastleigh was transferred back to BR ownership in April 1987, to become one of the three Level 5 facilities on the Southern Region.

During the mid-1980s the following Shops and buildings formed the Eastleigh Works complex:

Electrical Shop Repairs and overhaul of locomotives, coaching stock and vehicle electrical systems were all undertaken here, in addition to repairs to generators, traction motors and Signal & Telegraph equipment.

Diesel Engine Repair Shop This facility was responsible for cleaning, stripping, repairing and the reassembly of diesel engines, mainly from Classes 08, 09, 33, 73 and SR demu stock. Fuel injectors, turbochargers, exhausters and radiators were also maintained here.

Paint Shop Within this Shop all passenger and NPCCS vehicles had their bodies filled, primed, painted and finally lettered. The painting of locomotives usually being effected within the main Repair Shop as part of their classified overhaul programme.

Locomotive Erecting Shop This Shop, formed of a 3-track section within the main building, was responsible for all repairs to locomotives. Unlike other Works where locomotives visited various parts of the complex during repairs, at Eastleigh locomotives were usually stripped, repaired and repainted whilst in the one position.

Wheel Shop To the rear of the Locomotive Erecting Shop was the Wheel Shop which contained equipment for tyre turning, tyre boring, wheel assembly and wheel dynamic balancing. The fitting of roller bearings to axle boxes was also carried out in this Shop.

Carriage Repair Shop In BREL's latter days at Eastleigh the single most important duty was the repair of carriages, mainly of the emu and dmu type. The Carriage Shop was divided into four main sections:

1. The Body Shop: In which repairs to body sides, doors and interior fitments were carried out. The Body Shop was designed to operate on a flowline basis with a number of major items being removed from a vehicle at one end of the Shop, repaired and refitted to the same vehicle at the other.

2. The Sheet Metal Shop: Here steel or alloy panels and sections were formed into detail for body installation.

3. The Lifting Shop: In which high capacity overhead

cranes were provided, capable of lifting coaches off their bogies, thus enabling underframe equipment, brake and bogies to be overhauled.

4. The Trimming Shop: This section dealt with seat upholstery, curtains and floor coverings.

Machine Shop This Department undertook all general machining of new and repairable items, and also produced a sizeable amount of tooling for within the Works. The Shop was equipped with the latest electronically controlled lathes, drills, milling, slotting, screwing, shaping and planing machines, as well as a multihead flame cutter.

Plastic Shop With the increased use of plastic based products in coach building and repair, this Shop effected the manufacture of a number of preformed items.

Rewind Shop Situated adjacent to the Electrical Shop, the Rewind Shop provided modern facilities for coil winding and repair of motor armatures.

Van & Container Shop In this building repairs to coaching stock, vans (and at one time containers) was undertaken. In more recent years the Shop dealt with the major refurbishment programme of SR emus.

Saw Mill Situated to the rear of the Van Shop was the Works Saw Mill, which dealt with milling and preparation of timber for construction and repair work.

Diesel Test House Located at the far end of the Works Complex was the Test House, where all diesel locomotives including electro-diesels and the motor cars of SR demu stock passed, to check that all refitted equipment was working satisfactorily. In addition to the locomotive test facility a 2-track multiple unit test house was provided.

There were also sizeable carriage stabling sidings located to the rear of the Works used to store vehicles of sets whilst other cars were under repair. An asbestos removal facility was also provided at the rear of the Works, as was a coach detail inspection shed.

Other smaller Workshops located around the complex included the Millwright, Coppersmith, White Metal Shop. Smithy, Chain and Material. To provide easy vehicle movement between roads three traversers were to be found within the complex. One outside the front of the main Workshop and two within the stabling area.

A large office building together with a Canteen, Training School and First Aid post were provided near the main entrance.

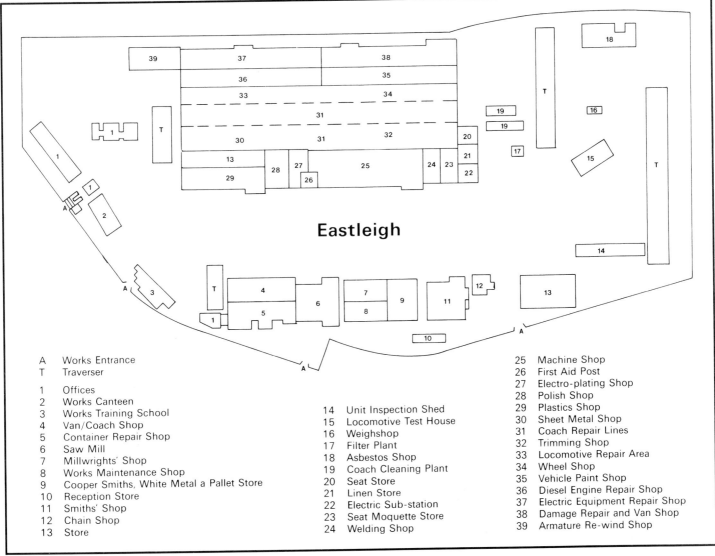

Eastleigh

A	Works Entrance	25	Machine Shop
T	Traverser	26	First Aid Post
		27	Electro-plating Shop
1	Offices	28	Polish Shop
2	Works Canteen	29	Plastics Shop
3	Works Training School	30	Sheet Metal Shop
4	Van/Coach Shop	14 Unit Inspection Shed	31	Coach Repair Lines
5	Container Repair Shop	15 Locomotive Test House	32	Trimming Shop
6	Saw Mill	16 Weighshop	33	Locomotive Repair Area
7	Millwrights' Shop	17 Filter Plant	34	Wheel Shop
8	Works Maintenance Shop	18 Asbestos Shop	35	Vehicle Paint Shop
9	Cooper Smiths, White Metal a Pallet Store	19 Coach Cleaning Plant	36	Diesel Engine Repair Shop
10	Reception Store	20 Seat Store	37	Electric Equipment Repair Shop
11	Smiths' Shop	21 Linen Store	38	Damage Repair and Van Shop
12	Chain Shop	22 Electric Sub-station	39	Armature Re-wind Shop
13	Store	23 Seat Moquette Store		
		24 Welding Shop		

A birdseye view of the Eastleigh Works complex:
1. Main office building. 2. Main entrance. 3. Works
Canteen. 4. Apprentice Training School. 5. Re-
wind Shop. 6. Inspection and Repair Control
Office. 7. Electrical Shop. 8. Locomotive Repair
Shop. 9. Wheel and Paint Shop. 10. Unit Repair
Shop. 11. Stores, Plastic and Polish Shop. 12.
Machine Shop. 13. Van Shop. 14. Container
Shop. 15. Test House. 16. Asbestos Plant.

Author's Collection

From the early 1960s, when BRCW Type 3
"Cromptons" were introduced, Eastleigh Works
was responsible for their classified attention. One
of the first to visit the Works was No. D6502 in
February 1961, when it received a power unit
change and minor collision repairs. The locomotive is seen having its replacement power unit
lowered into position.

Author's Collection

By virtue of its location and repair brief, Eastleigh Works saw the least number of locomotives of any BREL Locomotive Works, with during the 1980s, about seven being on works at any one time. This view of the main locomotive area on 25th April 1984 shows Class 73 Nos 73005 and 73131 and Class 33 No. 33003 receiving attention.

Colin J. Marsden

Unlike other works, locomotives visiting Eastleigh had all repair and painting work done in the one Shop. Whilst this was productive in the amount of workshop space occupied, all benefits were lost by the number of trades required to work in a confined area. This illustration shows a fitter repositioning a cab handrail on Class 33 No. 33029.

Colin J. Marsden

The Class 33 and 73 locomotives normally visited the Works every 4-5 years, however with the intense diagramming of the Class 73s on the "Gatwick Express" service, their new Level 5 shopping has been altered. The body of Class 73/1 No. 73131 is seen being prepared for painting in this April 1984 view.

Colin J. Marsden

To facilitate engine or bogie removal a 50 tonne overhead crane spanned the 3-road locomotive repair area. Class 33 Nos 33205, 33015 and 33023 are seen receiving intermediate/general overhauls in this August 1978 view. Providing no adverse delays occurred the Class 33s were usually 'out of traffic' for only between five and eight weeks, depending on the level of repair.

Colin J. Marsden

To provide testing after repairs, Eastleigh had a 2-track Test House containing sophisticated equipment to gauge locomotive performance. The upper illustration shows the rear end of the Test House which did not have a roof, but sound-insulated walls. Parked outside is former Southampton Docks shunter (Class 07) No. D2991 (now preserved), whilst the lower picture shows a Class 08 inside the Test House being prepared for main generator output testing.

Both: Colin J. Marsden

Following the introduction of Class 73s on the InterCity Sector's "Gatwick Express" service, it was decided to outshop the fleet in InterCity livery. Some examples were repainted by Stewarts Lane while others received their new livery at Eastleigh Works. No. 73137, sporting its new colours, poses inside the Locomotive Erecting Shop during final adjustments on 18th September 1985.

Colin J. Marsden

There was a sizeable Wheel Shop at Eastleigh Works which was equipped for tyre turning, boring and dynamic balancing. Here a set of wheels is seen being rotated at high speed during the balancing process.

J. Pike

In latter years the majority of suburban units to pass through Eastleigh were refurbished. This work included the complete 'gutting' of all vehicles and progressive refitting, using the latest style components. A tradesman is seen inspecting a roof detail prior to further reassembly of an EPB coach.

J. Pike

With the large number of passenger vehicles passing through the Works, a very active Trimming Shop, responsible for all upholstery and interior detail work, was provided. Seating moquette is seen being cut to size and sewn onto seat backs in this view.

J. Pike

In 1983-84 Eastleigh Works converted ten redundant 2HAP (Class 414) DMBS vehicles into Gatwick Luggage Vans (GLV) for the "Gatwick Express" service. The work involved the complete stripping of all interior items, altering the door arrangements and revising the drawgear equipment. The last car of the rebuild programme, DMBS of HAP No. 6082 is seen awaiting final testing and painting on 24th April 1984. When released to traffic this car became No. 9110.

Colin J. Marsden

As can be seen from this illustration, when vehicles were given facelift overhauls the amount of bodywork attention was quite considerable. The Driving Trailer of Class 416 No. 5677 shows that all doors and some windows were removed, together with many lower body panels that were obviously suffering from corrosion.

Colin J. Marsden

In recent years, with capacity being available at Eastleigh, a number of ER Class 302s were repaired here. The TC vehicle of unit No. 302208 is seen in the Paint Shop during body preparation. Note the safety scaffold in use.

Colin J. Marsden

The intermediate vehicle couplings of emu stock are normally of the buckeye or bar type, and therefore incompatible with shunting locomotives. This problem is overcome, when shunting is required, by the use of a matchwagon. One of Eastleigh match vehicles is seen attached to a 4CIG TS, while various vehicles of other emus are stabled in adjacent roads.

Colin J. Marsden

The main Coaching Stock Repair Shop operated on a flowline principle, with vehicles entering at the east end. This view shows the first stages of the flowline where internal stripping was effected, while underframe repairs have obviously already started.

Colin J. Marsden

One of the newer buildings at Eastleigh Works was the EMU Test House located to the east of the Works. This Shop, able to accommodate two 4-coach units simultaneously, carried out all electrical and brake testing. In this view a Class 302 is seen in the left bay, while a Class 422 is on the right.

Colin J. Marsden

To coincide with the 1986 Work's Open Day, held on 12th October 1986, withdrawn Class 07 No. D2991 was repainted into its original green livery with lion and wheel emblem on the cab sides. Being a credit to all those involved, the locomotive is seen stabled in the Works yard.

Colin J. Marsden

Glasgow

Only one BREL establishment existed north of the border – that of Glasgow, situated in the north east of the city in the Springburn district. BREL Glasgow occupied the former Caledonian Railway Company works at St Rollox, erected in 1856 for the construction of locomotives and stock which occupied a site of approximately 14 acres. The works was considerably enlarged in 1882 when the size increased to 31½ acres. Between 1882 and 1923 at the railway grouping, St Rollox constructed many hundreds of steam locomotives, passenger coaches and goods wagons, effecting repairs to many thousands of similar items for the Caledonian Railway. In 1927 there was a complete reorganisation of the Works under the LMS, with the cessation of new locomotive building, and the wagon operation, involving construction and repair work, being transferred to Barassie Works, St Rollox being solely responsible for repairs to locomotives and coaches.

Upon Nationalisation in January 1948 the British Transport Commission (BTC) acquired several workshops in Scotland and for a time all were kept occupied. However by the early 1960s rumours were rife that several workshops would be closed and possibly in the long term, only one would survive. Major reorganisation of the Scottish workshops did not occur however until 1964-68, leading to the closure of the former North British Cowlairs Works in Glasgow, and the amalgamation of the St Rollox and Cowlairs workload and workforce. The Wagon Works at Barassie surprisingly survived under the BTC/BR flag until 1972, (although not taken over by BREL) when it finally closed. The former Great North of Scotland Railway works at Inverurie was also closed. By this time the St Rollox name was dropped and the Works identified as 'Glasgow Works', which took over all wagon repairs and modifications, as well as dealing with coach and traction items.

Following the introduction of diesel traction to the Scottish Region in the early 1960s, Glasgow's main undertaking was classified overhauls of shunting and main line diesel locomotives, emu, dmu, and loco-hauled vehicles. In the mid-1960s locomotives of Classes 06, 08, 17, 20, 21, 24, 25, 26, 27 and 29 were regular visitors to the Works for overhaul. However, by 1987 when the Works was transferred back to BR as the Scottish Region's Springburn Level 5 depot under the control of BRML, the workload was considerably less. Over the years the Works carried out a number of dual brake conversions to Classes 20, 26 and 27, which did secure a short time reprieve for some of the workforce.

Apart from locomotives, Glasgow Works has undertaken classified overhauls on the Scottish Region allocated Class 303 and 311 emus, including a major refurbishing programme in latter years. Overhauls were also carried out on a number of the Region's dmu vehicles, but in more recent times this operation reduced. The majority of ScR coaches were also maintained and modified by the Works, and the most notable achievement in this field was the conversion of the Driving Brake Second Open (DBSO) vehicles for the Edinburgh-Glasgow push-pull service from Brake Second Open (BSO) stock during the early and mid-1980s.

The Works complex in more recent years covered an area of 42 acres of which some 20 acres were under cover. The workforce in August 1985 stood at just 400.

Although wagon repairs were taken over at Glasgow when Barassie Works closed in 1972, by the mid-1980s this work had ceased, as had the repairs to lifting tackle, S&T Department relays and container maintenance. All wagon overhauls were then transferred to Shildon and Doncaster.

Towards the end of the BREL operation at Glasgow the following main Shops were provided, the Works basically consisting of one main building divided into various Shops, and several smaller out-buildings:

Coach Repair Shop This Shop housed a special 70 ton lifting traverser, allowing coaches to be lifted and moved for Bogie underside overhaul. When vehicles arrived they were normally positioned on special accommodation bogies, these being at a suitable working height. Side platforms were also provided to ease access. The Shop had accommodation for 20 coaches in ten workings bays.

DMU Engine Repair Shop Complete overhauls and repairs to diesel engines, fluid flywheels, gear boxes and final drives were effected in this Shop. Components were cleaned prior to repair by means of 'Ardrox' tanks, a hot tunnel wash and hot spray booth. Pendant control overhead cranes served this maintenance area to lift or lower units onto manipulators for support whilst overhaul was carried out.

Fitting & Wheel Shop These two Shops, grouped together, looked after the overhaul and repair of rolling stock sub-assemblies, ie compressors, exhausters and turbo-blowers. The wheel section undertook tyre turning, boring, retyring, dynamic balancing and ultra-sonic flaw detection. A special 600 ton press was provided for installing wheels onto their axles.

Machine Shop Activities here included turning, milling, drilling, planing and grinding operations. A number of the machines installed were of the latest electronic computer controlled types, producing a high daily output. An amount of products from this Shop were supplied to other works and BR depots.

Main Erecting Shop It was within this Shop that all diesel locomotives and some emu coaches were stripped, repaired and refitted. High capacity overhead cranes were installed for movement of vehicles, which had the capability to lift a complete locomotive.

Electrical Shop To the rear of the Main Erecting Shop was the Electrical Shop where generators, motors and loco/unit control panels, as well as auxiliary motors, were overhauled.

Smithy & Spring Shop The Smithy Shop contained pneumatic hammers for the shaping of forgings, while the Spring Shop used a progressive system to examine and test every spring passing through the Works. Facilities existed for heat treatment normalizing and case hardening.

Trimming Shop Located alongside the Coach Repair Shop, this section refurbished coach upholstery, coach internal electrics and detail fitments.

Plating & Fabrication Shop All types of plating and metal fabrication work were undertaken in this Shop. The main operations included plate rolling, bending and the cutting of sheet steel to size. The Fabrication Section was fully equipped with modern electric and gas welding equipment, and a multi-head flame cutting system was also provided.

Diesel Test House A 2-track Diesel Test House was

provided for thorough testing of all repaired locomotives. The section was completely soundproofed with a separate control cabin.

Paint Shop This small outstation to the main Works building was fitted with spray equipment for coach finishing. Movement between roads was by traverser.

Asbestos Shop Another of the outstations was the Asbestos Shop which had special equipment for the removal of asbestos lining found in older type vehicles. Near clinical conditions existed within this Shop to ensure that no asbestos dust escaped into the atmosphere. Staff working in this area had to wear 'space suits' to meet Health & Safety requirements.

EMU/DMU Test House A sizeable EMU/DMU Test House was provided which undertook full brake, power and insulation testing to unit stock.

Other smaller shops such as the Millwrights, Welding, Boiler, Battery and Traction Electrics were provided around the complex giving essential support services to the main activities.

Offices, Accounts Section and Supplies Unit were provided near the Charles Street gate, together with a Works Training School, Staff Canteen and Welfare facility.

Following the 1987 BREL alterations, and the handing over of the Glasgow site to BR to form the Springburn Level 5 Depot of the DM&EE operated BR Maintenance Group, virtually all Scottish allocated traction and rolling stock came under the supervision of this depot, including Class 47 locomotives for CEM overhauls.

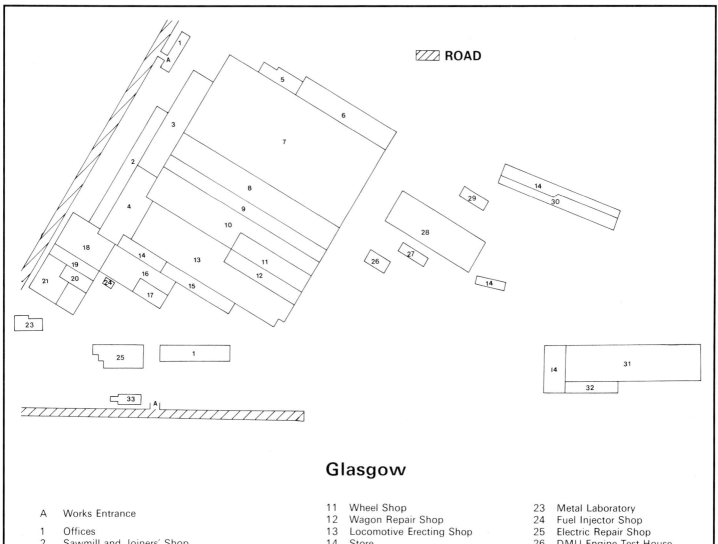

Glasgow

A	Works Entrance	11	Wheel Shop	23	Metal Laboratory
1	Offices	12	Wagon Repair Shop	24	Fuel Injector Shop
2	Sawmill and Joiners' Shop	13	Locomotive Erecting Shop	25	Electric Repair Shop
3	Smithy and Spring Shop	14	Store	26	DMU Engine Test House
4	Electrics Shop	15	Staff Amenities	27	Asbestos Shop
5	Staff Canteen	16	Crane Shop	28	Paint Shop
6	Trimming Shop and Coach Electricians' Shop	17	Locomotive Test House	29	Battery Shop
7	Coach Repair Shop	18	Plating and Fabrication Shop	30	Unit Test House
8	DMU Engine Repair Shop	19	Welding Shop	31	Container Shop
9	Fitting Shop	20	Training School	32	Signal and Telegraph Shop
10	Machine Shop	21	Millwrights' Shop	33	Laboratory
		22	Boiler House		

An aerial view of Glasgow St Rollox Works, prior to the 1964 modernisation scheme.

In recent years BREL Glasgow was responsible for the overhaul of Classes 08, 20, 26 and 27 locomotives. This general view of the 2-bay locomotive erecting area shows various members of Classes 08, 20, 26 and 27 locomotives under repair during 1974.

Two 50 ton capacity overhead gantry cranes spanned the locomotive repair bays. They were quite capable of lifting most locomotive classes clear of the rails, as demonstrated in this view of a Class 20 body being moved down the shop following repair. Several other members of Classes 08, 25, 26 and 27 can be observed in the Shop.

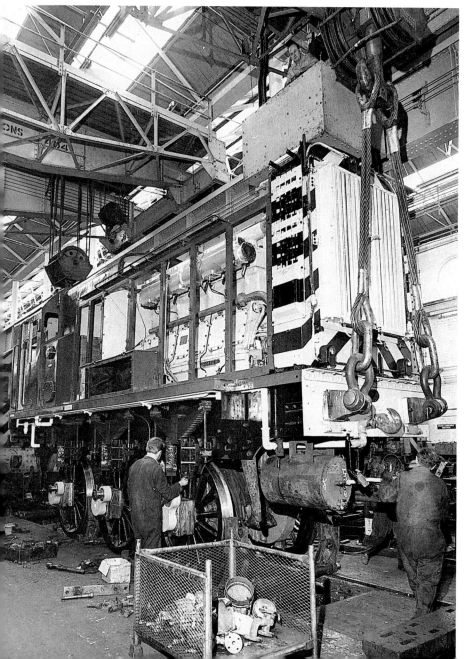

The Scottish allocated Class 08s were usually maintained at Glasgow Works and following the rundown of Swindon saw a slightly increased shunter workload. Here, two overhead cranes slowly lower a Class 08 body back onto its wheelsets in June 1974 whilst a general overhaul is carried out.

This view shows part of Glasgow Works taken in January 1977, and depicts the Locomotive Test House (on the right), with various now-obsolete Class 25 and 27 locomotives present. In the foreground part of the Works' administration facility can be seen. The four tall chimneys on the left are part of the Works' boiler house.

Tom Noble

With some of Glasgow's high-rise flats forming a backdrop, two Class 26s and a Class 08 stand outside the Test area in this 1980 view. During the early 1980s a number of Class 26s passed through the Works for classified and refurbishing overhauls.

Tom Noble

Prior to the general rundown of the Works on grounds of economy, a visitor could expect to find some 20 main line, and five shunting locomotives under repair at any one time, but alas today under the control of the BRMG it is a very different story. In this view, when the building was under BREL control, the near empty Erecting Shop houses only two Class 26 and one Class 08.

Tom Noble

In April/May 1976 privately owned A4 Class 4-6-2 No. 60009 *Union of South Africa* visited the Works for tyre turning and other essential maintenance. This work was carried out on behalf of the locomotive's owner, who contracted BREL to effect repairs. This view shows the locomotive together with a withdrawn Class 25/0 adjacent to the Work's wheel store.

Tom Noble

One section of the main Works building was dedicated to the repair of dmu engines, for both Works and Depot use. A dmu engine camshaft is seen here being reassembled. Note the weight is being borne by an overhead crane.

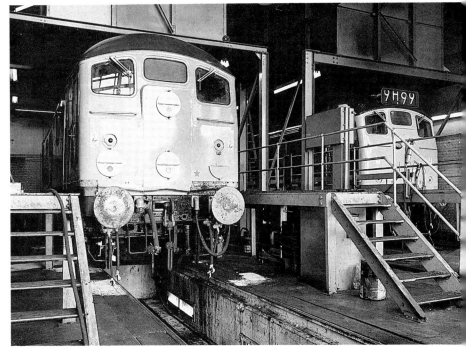

A 2-berth locomotive Testing Station was provided at BRE Glasgow Works. This normally dealt with locomotives that had been technically repaired, and to ensure that all components performed correctly the machines were put through their paces. An active road test trial was also conducted, normally in tandem with a traffic locomotive. Two Class 24s are seen sharing space in the test area on 5th June 1974.

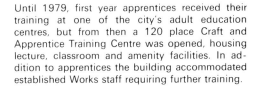

Until 1979, first year apprentices received their training at one of the city's adult education centres, but from then a 120 place Craft and Apprentice Training Centre was opened, housing lecture, classroom and amenity facilities. In addition to apprentices the building accommodated established Works staff requiring further training.

When a decision was made to revamp the lucrative Edinburgh-Glasgow high speed InterCity route a fleet of Driving Trailer Cars was required to operate at the remote ends of trains powered by Class 47/7s, using the RCH method of control. Glasgow Works was given the task of converting a fleet of Mk IIf Brake Second Open (BSO) cars into Driving Brake Second Open (DBSO). The first complete DBSO No. 9701 is illustrated from the driving end.

Colin J. Marsden

Previously modernised Class 26/0 No. 26007, devoid of its centre doorway, stands in the Works yard on 5th November 1987, painted in Railfreight livery.

Maxwell H. Fowler

Inside the main workshop, HA allocated Class 20 No. 20213 receives power unit, bogie and underframe repairs. The locomotive is standing on special stands whilst the bogies receive attention in another shop.

Maxwell H. Fowler

For many years Glasgow was responsible for virtually all Scottish Region allocated loco-hauled passenger and NPCCS stock. Here we see Mk I SK No. SC18819 awaiting attention in the Works yard during Spring 1984.

David Nicholas

The Scottish Region allocated Class 303/311 fleet has always been a major part of the Glasgow workload. Strathclyde liveried Class 303 units are seen in the Carriage Repair Shop receiving refurbishment.

Maxwell H. Fowler

BREL was also deployed on the breaking up of several withdrawn locomotives during its reign at Glasgow. In this view Class 20 No. 20207 stands awaiting the cutter's torch following collision damage in 1984.

David Nicholas

In the early 1970s, when the Liberian Mining Company (Lamco) was in need of rolling stock for its network, BR offered a fleet of former InterCity dmmu Driving Cars for sale. Lamco purchased this stock, but prior to departure the vehicles were given classified overhauls at Glasgow Works. One of the completed vehicles is seen being loaded onto the deck of a cargo vessel for its long journey to Liberia.

Following the transfer to BREL Glasgow to BR Maintenance Ltd, the complex started to receive Class 47s for CEM. In this May 1988 view Class 47/7 No. 47711 *Greyfriars Bobby* is seen inside the main shop receiving bogie attention.

Maxwell H. Fowler

In addition to working for BR, the Springburn depot of BRML has carried out work for the private sector. This has included the almost total rebuild of Class 27 No. D5394 for the Strathspey Railway. When complete the locomotive was outshopped in BR green livery with small yellow warning panels.

Maxwell H. Fowler

Horwich

BREL Horwich Works, situated six miles north of Bolton in Lancashire, was built in 1885 by the Lancashire & Yorkshire Railway Company (LYR) for the manufacture and repair of locomotives and rolling stock. As the railway manufacturing industry expanded in the late 19th century, Horwich Works was enlarged, with many new Shops being added between 1887 and 1900. The LYR Works continued in its original form until January 1923 when the Grouping of railway companies prevailed, bringing Horwich under the control of the LMS. In the immediate years after Grouping the Works continued in its role as a manufacturer and repairer of locomotives and rolling stock.

From January 1948 Horwich Works came under the control of the British Transport Commission and later BR, forming part of the BR Workshops Division. During the 1950s, with the advent of the diesel age, Horwich was entrusted with the construction of a significant batch of the standard 0-6-0 diesel electric shunter type.

Horwich diesel build:

Number Range	Total	Years
D3593-D3607	15	1958
D3803-D3831	29	1959
D3842-D3871	30	1959-60
D3922-D3936	15	1961
D4011-D4027	17	1961
D4095-D4157	63	1961-62

Although Horwich Works had locomotive building facilities, and had demonstrated their modern traction abilities, no construction contracts were forthcoming following the above shunter builds, the Works being thus deemed as a major repair facility.

After the demise of steam traction, the Works concentrated on carriage and wagon operations: on the coach front the Works became responsible for a number of Mk I vehicles as well as emus of Classes 502, 503, 504, 506 and latterly Classes 313, 314 and 507. Wagon operations consisted of the construction of new types and repairs to a number of revenue fleet vehicles, but in latter years the emphasis was placed on Departmental stock and conversion work. In the late 1970s and early 1980s a large number of overhead electrification maintenance coaches were converted from Mk I passenger stock.

As well as undertaking overhauls on emu classes listed above, between 1979 and 1983 a substantial number of SR 4EPB sets were 'facelifted' at the Works. This involved the opening out of compartment vehicles and bringing internal decor up to the latest standards, including the installation of fluorescent lighting and a public address system. The EPB 'facelift' programme also included the conversion of a number of former 4SUB, Class 405 trailer vehicles to EPB standards, by the fitting of electro-pneumatic brake equipment and complete interior rebuilding.

During the early 1980s a number of withdrawn emu and loco-hauled vehicles were broken up at the Works. This contract included several Class 306 emus from the ER, together with 4SUB and 2SAP stock from the Southern.

In addition to carrying out repairs to passenger and freight stock, Horwich was also responsible for repairing some Civil Engineering plant, this included ballast cleaning machines, tamping machines and track relayers. In addition to repairs to railborne vehicles, activities included PVC, nylon and polyester manufacture, laminated steel assembly, iron casting and container repairs.

The large iron foundry was capable of producing some 42,000 tons per annum and was the major foundry within the BREL group, supplying not only BREL but BR with a number of cast requirements. Following the closure of the main Works during the mid-1980s the iron foundry remained in operation, although in a lesser form, and was sold at the end of 1987 as a going concern.

In the immediate years leading up to closure the following major shops formed the Works:

Carriage Repair Shop It was within the environs of this Shop that all coach repairs, modifications and rebuilding took place, including work on loco-hauled and emu vehicles. Shop facilities included four 30 ton overhead cranes.

Wagon Repair Shop This was the largest shop within the Works, occupying an area of 1,240ft in length by 118ft in width. Internally it was arranged in two long bays, each sub-divided into three sections by two traversing tables. The specialist work undertaken was primarily to steel bodied wagons, ie minerals or coal hoppers. It was also equipped for new wagon construction contracts. Twelve overhead lifting cranes were provided.

Wheel Shop The Wheel Shop was responsible for reconditioning wagon wheels removed from stock arriving at the Works, in addition to those brought in from regional depots. Maintenance was also performed on emu wheelsets. Facilities existed within the Shop for replacement fitting of wheels, tyres, gears and axles. Specialised equipment included wheel reprofiling lathes, axle turning and burnishing machines and ultra-sonic floor detection equipment.

Paint Shop This small building was used for the painting of all new and repaired stock, most body painting being effected by modern airless spray equipment, drying was assisted by warm air blowers.

Sheet Shop It was here that the production of PVC/nylon, canvass and polyester sheeting was carried out.

Millwrights' Shop It was the responsibility of this Shop to maintain all 'on works' plant and, in addition, to overhaul some Chief Civil Engineers' (CCE) crane equipment.

Pattern & Joinery Shop All patterns used in the Works foundries were supplied and maintained by this Shop. A small section was used by the joiners mainly for Works maintenance.

Machine Shop This Shop was equipped with the usual array of grinding, drilling, milling, planing and slotting machines. A tool room formed part of the building for the manufacture of Works tooling and jigs.

Wood Machine Shop This department was equipped with high speed wood preparation equipment, the products of which were used for coach and wagon construction and repair. A special sawdust extractor system was provided to improve the working environment.

Mobile Plant Shop This facility undertook the majority of repair work on CCE railmounted machines, including tamping, ballast cleaners and track relayer units. Diesel engines from some plant was also overhauled here.

Container, Plating & Fabrication Shop This building was divided into north and south bays: the north bay carrying out construction and maintenance of Freightliner containers for BR and the private sector, while the south bay effected general plating and fabrication work.

Mechanized Foundry This was one of the most modern foundries in Europe manufacturing such items as brake blocks, track base plates, chairs and many other items for the Civil Engineering and Mechanical Engineering Departments.

Iron Foundry This was a self-contained unit specializing in greensand plate pattern moulding, providing castings for virtually every sphere of the railway industry.

Press/Smithy/Spring Shops This group of three small shops was concerned with the production of steel backplates and clips for brake blocks, the production of buffing and drawgear, and the manufacturer of various springs. When in full operation the plant was able to produce 1,500 new springs per week and repair another 300.

Other smaller shops found at the Works were: Container Paint Shop, Sheet Metal Shop, Heat Treatment Shop, Electrical Maintenance Shop, Test Room and Stores.

To deal with any medical problems the Works had a resident nursing sister on duty at all times, and a Group Medical Officer who called at the Works twice a week. In common with all BREL Works there were sizeable administration buildings, a Works Training School, a Canteen and of course social facilities.

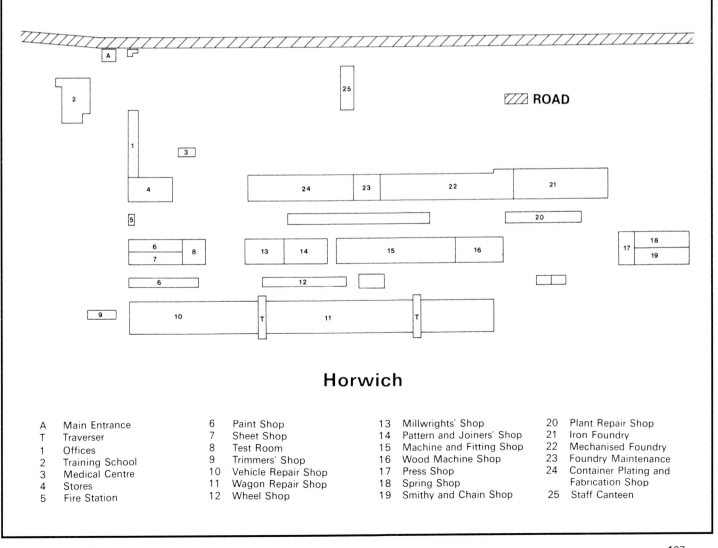

Horwich

A	Main Entrance	6	Paint Shop	13	Millwrights' Shop	20	Plant Repair Shop
T	Traverser	7	Sheet Shop	14	Pattern and Joiners' Shop	21	Iron Foundry
1	Offices	8	Test Room	15	Machine and Fitting Shop	22	Mechanised Foundry
2	Training School	9	Trimmers' Shop	16	Wood Machine Shop	23	Foundry Maintenance
3	Medical Centre	10	Vehicle Repair Shop	17	Press Shop	24	Container Plating and
4	Stores	11	Wagon Repair Shop	18	Spring Shop		Fabrication Shop
5	Fire Station	12	Wheel Shop	19	Smithy and Chain Shop	25	Staff Canteen

In the years leading up to eventual closure of Horwich Works, a major undertaking was the repair and modernisation of emus. As the lines to and from the works were not electrified, stock was usually marshalled between match wagons and hauled to the complex. Here ER unit No. 313046 stands in the Works reception area awaiting admittance on 3rd October 1981.

Colin J. Marsden

One of the Works' pilots, Class 08 No. 08273 stands adjacent to a traverser outside the main shop. Class 503 DMBS No. M28376M now withdrawn, is also visible on one of the traverser sidings. The traverser itself was over 60ft long and able to accommodate most loco-hauled and emu vehicles.

Colin J. Marsden

To provide the M&EE with modern overhead line maintenance trains, a fleet of 'flat top' vehicles were converted from redundant Mk I stock between 1979 and 1982. The work involved the removal of the original coach roof, fitting a flat roof height platform and roof-mounted inspection lighting. In this aerial view five 'flat tops' are seen under conversion in the Carriage Repair Shop.
Colin J. Marsden

The 'flat top' conversion contract also called for the provision of new vehicle ends, incorporating slim width doors and end ladders. The 'flat top' conversion illustrated here was formerly a Mk I BSK.

Colin J. Marsden

Painted in distinctive Departmental olive green livery with black and yellow chevron ends, and bearing the legend *Not to be hump or loose shunted*, a completed dual brake 'flat top' receives its finishing touches. Each 'flat top' conversion took approximately twelve weeks to complete.

In conjunction with the SR Class 415 'facelift' programme, which included the DMBS vehicles of SR design 2SAP stock, the DTS cars became redundant and scrapped at Horwich Works, after all re-usable components had been removed. SAP DTS No. S14538S from unit number 5618 awaits dismantling in the Works' scrap area.
Colin J. Marsden

If vehicles arrived at Horwich with damaged or defective bogies these were normally removed with some urgency, thus enabling their repair to commence. To permit vehicle movement around the Works coaches were mounted on accommodation bogies, these sometimes being purpose-built wheelsets or reclaimed bogies from withdrawn stock. 'Bury' DTS No. M77174 is seen supported at one end by its correct bogie and at the other by a trolley.
Colin J. Marsden

General view inside the Wagon Repair Shop, taken in September 1980, showing two goods brakevans and a 12 ton box van under repair. The large electrically powered overhead crane can be seen at the far end with the operator's cabin to the right.

One of the smaller outstations at the Works was the Spring Shop which catered for the progressive manufacture of various spring types. This picture shows an 11-leaf spring being lifted by electric hoist into the Test Bed, a most important part of the spring assembly process, bearing in mind that coach or wagon stability and thus human life will depend upon the springs.

In the late 1970s/early 1980s, when the SR was badly in need of updated suburban stock, the Works took part in a major 'facelift' programme of the EPB fleet. This work included the opening out of compartment vehicles and general modernisation. DMBS of unit number 5224 is pictured on works accommodation stands during the early stages of refurbishment. When this car eventually departed from the Works it formed one of the Driving vehicles of unit number 5424.

Colin J. Marsden

The internal work incurred in the SR EPB 'facelift' programme was considerable and in each case necessitated the stripping of all internal fittings. The progressive refitting work included new lower ceilings housing fluorescent lighting, new design coach heaters and reupholstered seats. The interior of a DMBS car is shown.

Colin J. Marsden

The Horwich 'facelift' EPBs were finished to a high standard, both in terms of coach building and electric installation. Considering that the Works did not have a 'live rail' for testing, the number of electrical problems recorded that had to be rectified by the SR were very few. Cars of set number 5234, which become 'facelifted' set number 5422, are shown.

Colin J. Marsden

Although the 1972 derivative high density stock types were built at BREL York Works, Horwich became responsible for classified overhauls on selected Class 313s, 314s and some 507s. Here Class 313 set No. 313005 split into its three constituent cars, stands on 'high' accommodation bogies in the Main Shop whilst underside repairs are carried out.

The Wolverton built Class 504 Manchester-Bury units were always repaired at Horwich until closure, usually visiting the Works for classified attention at 4-5 yearly intervals. This illustration shows trailer vehicle No. M77165 in March 1974 undergoing heavy overhaul.

Some of the most important items within each Works are the overhead cranes permitting easy movement of vehicles and components within the buildings. In 1981 two John Smith 25 tonne overhead cranes were installed in the Horwich Carriage Repair Shop, illustrated soon after fitting. Various Mk I and Mk II coaches can be seen around the Shop.
John Smith Ltd

During the late 1970s preserved 'Western' Class No. D1048 *Western Lady* was stored, out of use at BREL Horwich. This locomotive is now in the process of restoration on the Bodmin & Wenford Railway in Cornwall.
Colin J. Marsden

Shildon

The Railway Works at Shildon was established in 1833 by the Stockton & Darlington Railway Company (S&DR), primarily for the manufacture and repair of locomotives. With the rapid growth of the railway industry the Works soon found that its major role was in the production and maintenance of rolling stock as well as traction, this becoming the major works operation from the mid-1860s for over a hundred years.

The initial Shildon Works complex occupied a site of just ten acres, but over the years additional land was purchased and by 1970 a site of 55 acres belonged to the Works. Shildon came under the control of the London & North Eastern Railway Company (LNER) from the Grouping in 1923, and the BTC/BR from January 1948. The Works eventually formed part of the BREL Group from 1970. In the five years prior to the formation of BREL, the Works was extensively modernised and geared for modern wagon assembly, modification and repair work. From 1970 the Works was divided into two main categories – that of repair and new build. The 1970 workforce stood at just over 2,600 which was equally divided between the two operations.

During the early 1970s, when BR placed significant investment in new wagon types, the Works played a major role in producing thousands of new vehicles, while at the same time responsibility for classified attention of 60% of the active wagon fleet was retained. In addition to general repair work, Shildon had the endless task of rebodying many hundreds of existing wagons and adapting vehicles to meet customer requirements.

Over the years since the first unbraked chaldron wagons were produced at Shildon for the S&DR, wagon construction became a complex operation, raising the need for much additional workshop space, special tooling, and the use of computer controlled design and assembly equipment.

As well as supplying BR with wagon stock, the Works manufactured many hundreds of vehicles for the private sector, some being standard 'off the shelf' designs but the majority were purpose designed vehicles for an identified use.

The largest BR wagon order placed with the Works was for the HAA/HDA hopper wagons for mgr operation – a staggering number in excess of 10,000 being built between 1964 and 1977. Other sizeable British contracts have included assembly of Presflo, Freightliner and numerous van types. In addition to producing wagons for the British market the Works built several hundreds for export. Countries operating Shildon products included Malaya, Kenya, Ghana, Jordan, Nigeria, Tanzania, Yugoslavia, Zambia, Bangladesh, and the Republic of Ireland.

To mark the 150th anniversary of the opening of the Stockton & Darlington Railway in 1975, a cavalcade of ancient and modern motive power was held. Shildon Works played host to most of the steam exhibits and the BREL site was opened to the public.

Unfortunately, with declining new build contracts and revised working practices, BREL decided to close the Works with effect from the end of 1984. The workforce, of course, strongly opposed such closure plans and along with Trade Unions and local community officials protested locally and nationally, but all to no avail, and Shildon's association with rail transport ended after over 150 years.

In the period immediately prior to closure, the following Shops were to be found at the Works:

Bogie Vehicle Repair Shop This Shop had facilities for repair, modification and conversion of bogie goods vehicles, with two 12 ton overhead cranes being provided.

Wagon Repair Shop This 5-road Shop carried out repairs to steel bodied vehicles and was laid out for a progressive flow-line system. Three of the five roads were equipped with deep pits, and the Shop was served by overhead cranes.

Machine Shop & Tool Room The Machine Shop provided for the general machining of metal components for both new build and repair work. This Department housed some of the most modern computer controlled milling, drilling and turning machines found at any BREL Works. Adjoining the Machine Shop was the Works Tool Room which produced and manufactured jigs and templates. Modern hydro-copying machines, together with spark erosion facilities produced the forging and drop stamp dyes.

Plate & Section Shop This Department processed around 20,000 tons of steel each year for use in new build and repair work. Facilities installed were a high capacity 400 ton press, large steel cutting guillotines and a number of multi-head flame cutters with capacity to cut material from $1^1/2$in to 30in thickness.

New Wagon Construction Shop This shop was again designed for progressive flow-line work, building all types of fixed wheel and bogie vehicles. A 60ft manipulator was installed as were boom arm automatic welding units. There were also a number $7^1/2$, 15 and 25 ton overhead cranes.

Smiths' Shop This had a section for the blacksmith's trade and another for flash-butt welding. This Shop adjoined the Wagon Repair Shop.

Forge & Press Shop There were facilities here for drop stamping and upset forging which, together with associated trimming presses gave the shop capacity to deal with items up to 5 tons. A hydraulic 350 ton press was installed for pressing plate work associated with wagon construction, the steel being heated by gas fired furnaces.

Fabrication Shop The object of this section was to provide the Construction Shop with welded components and assemblies so a number of special fabrication jigs were installed.

Paint Shop Adjacent to the Fabrication Shop was the Paint Shop where airless spray equipment was extensively used. One section of the Shop was used for sign-writing and the production of silk screens for wagon labelling.

Final Assembly Shop This Shop provided facilities for the final construction stage detailed fitting, including door and brake fixtures.

Lift & Brake Shop Special facilities existed in this Shop for the lifting of vehicle bodies for wheel, suspension and brake gear replacement.

Wheel Shop A sizeable Wheel Shop was provided being able to undertake all repairs to wheels and axles including turning and reprofiling. Ultra-sonic axle test equipment was also installed.

In addition to the main Shops described, various Stores, Works Maintenance Units, Offices, Heat Treatment Shop and Training School were provided. Staff amenities included a Canteen and Social Club.

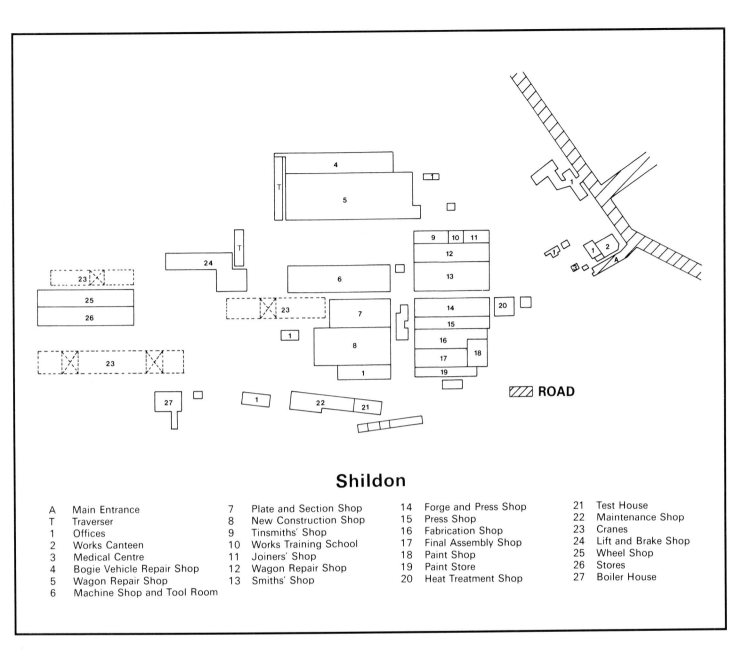

Shildon

A	Main Entrance	7	Plate and Section Shop	14	Forge and Press Shop	21	Test House
T	Traverser	8	New Construction Shop	15	Press Shop	22	Maintenance Shop
1	Offices	9	Tinsmiths' Shop	16	Fabrication Shop	23	Cranes
2	Works Canteen	10	Works Training School	17	Final Assembly Shop	24	Lift and Brake Shop
3	Medical Centre	11	Joiners' Shop	18	Paint Shop	25	Wheel Shop
4	Bogie Vehicle Repair Shop	12	Wagon Repair Shop	19	Paint Store	26	Stores
5	Wagon Repair Shop	13	Smiths' Shop	20	Heat Treatment Shop	27	Boiler House
6	Machine Shop and Tool Room						

A general view of Shildon Works yard showing the main Wagon Repair Shop on the right, and the Fabrication and Assembly Shops towards the left. In the yards are a number of bogie flat, coal hopper, mineral and box vans awaiting attention.

The most numerous wagon fleet produced at Shildon was the mgr coal hopper of type HAA. In addition to a near continual production run of the type for well over ten years, an on-going contract was placed with the Works for the rebodying of existing vehicles. HAA No. 368352 built in 1975 is seen here in November 1980 during rebodying.

Shildon Works assisted with the BREL export drive, producing several batches of export vehicles. One of the first orders received after the formation of the Company in January 1970, was placed on 24th February 1970 for metre gauge bogie pallet wagons for the Malayan Railways. The first completed vehicle is illustrated in the Works before departure.

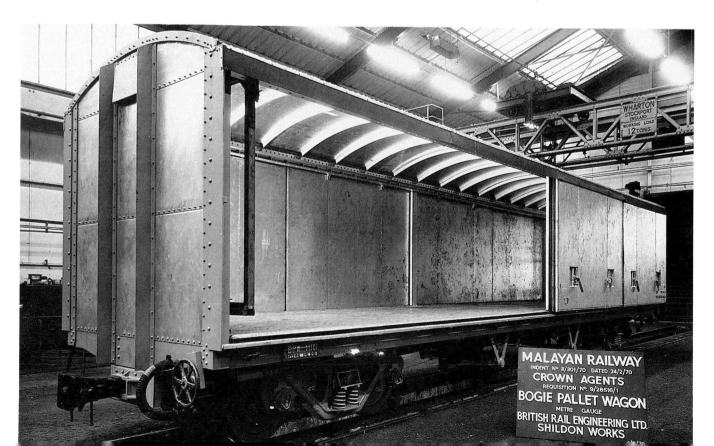

BREL Shildon was closed during 1984, with the total loss of jobs, thus causing much bitter feeling among local residents of an area already suffering from high unemployment. Nevertheless, BR decided to name IC125 power car no. 43078 *Shildon County Durham* to mark the town's long association with the railway industry.

Colin J. Marsden

A 1952 Shildon product, 24¹/₂ton coal hopper No. B333000, an experimental vehicle constructed to lot No. 2504.

Colin J. Marsden

Swindon

Probably the most famous of any BREL Works was that of Swindon, which alas is now no more. With the formation of the Great Western Railway (GWR) in 1840, the need of a works for locomotives, rolling stock and plant was apparent. The area of Swindon was chosen for the Company's main works and a site on the north side of the London-Bristol line was purchased. By 1843 the Works was fully operational and employed around 400 staff, of which 72 were skilled engineers.

At first only locomotive work was performed, but in 1869 considerable expansion took place and a Carriage and Wagon Section opened. From then the Swindon Works complex gradually grew until in 1930 the site occupied was in excess of 300 acres. In the intervening years many hundreds of famous GWR locomotives were constructed, as well as thousands of carriages and wagons. Swindon continued the building of steam right to the very end, when in 1960 the Works completed the final steam locomotive for BR – Class 9F 2-10-0 No. 92220 *Evening Star.* This machine was turned out in true Great Western tradition, painted in lined green livery and having the famous copper-capped chimney.

Swindon s association with diesel traction commenced in 1948 when a fleet of six 0-6-0 diesel electric shunters were constructed. The modern traction era continued in future years with such famous classes as the 'Warships' and 'Westerns' being assembled.

Swindon Works diesel building:

Class	Type	Total	Years
*	0-6-0	6	1948
**	0-6-0	1	1949
03	0-6-0	148	1957-61
14	0-6-0	56	1964-65
42	B-B	38	1960-61
52	C-C	30	1951-64

* Locomotive numbers 15101-15106.
** Locomotive number 15107.

Type	Number Range	Total	Year
DMS(L)	50647-50695	49	1957
DMBC	50696-50744	49	1957
DMS(L)	50936	1	1959
DMS(L)	51008-51029	22	1959
DMBS(L)	51030-51051	22	1959
DMBC(L)	51573-51581	9	1961
DMS(L)	51582-51590	9	1961
DMBC	51781-51787	7	1959
DMS(L)	51788-51794	7	1959
DMC	51951-51967	17	1960
DMBC	51968-51984	17	1960
DMBS(L)	52086-52095	10	1963
DMS	52096-52105	10	1963
TBF(L)	59098-59099	2	1961
TS(L)	59235-59239	5	1963
TBS(L)	59255-59301	47	1958
TF.	59391-59400	10	1959
TC(L)	59402-59412	11	1959
TBS(L)	59579-59588	10	1960
TBS(L)	59679-59685	7	1959
TS(L)	59765-59773	9	1960
TBF(L)	59774-59781	8	1960
TC	59818-59827	10	1963
TBS	59828-59832	5	1963
DMBS(L)	79083-79111	29	1956
DMS(L)	59155-59168	14	1957
TBF	79440-79447	8	1957
TF	79470-79482	13	1957

As well as all the above construction Swindon undertook major maintenance and assembly work on carriage and wagon stock, in addition to scrapping hundreds of steam locomotives in the early 1960s.

From 1962 the Works, by now under the auspices of the BTC, was the subject of a major reorganisation under the National Workshops Plan. This brought about the closure of the original Carriage and Wagon Plant and the almost total rebuilding of the locomotive section. The operation took nearly five years to complete and cost over £2$\frac{1}{2}$ million. When completed it left the Works responsible for repairing and modifying existing locomotive fleets, diesel unit stock, passenger coaches, NPCCS vehicles and a few wagons.

On the diesel repair side, the Works was specially geared to undertake diesel hydraulic overhauls and understandably as the diesel hydraulic fleet gradually diminished in size, so did Swindon Work's load. Passenger stock overhauls remained fairly constant during the early 1960s but as traffic fleets reduced this too reflected in the Works input.

After the BREL takeover from 1st January 1970, the Works main brief was then the repair of coaches and unit stock only, as by the early 1970s the hydraulic era was almost over, with only a handful of repairs left and the only major hydraulic undertaking remaining was the scrapping of virtually all machines. For a number of years Swindon had been responsible for selected dmu stock, primarily that allocated to the WR, however soon after the BREL formation, plans were announced for the refurbishment of almost the entire ageing dmmu fleet – Swindon being awarded a sizeable proportion of this lucrative contract.

In 1978-79 the Southern Region authorised a major refurbishing programme for its CEP/BEP (Class 411/412 emu fleet), with Swindon Works being awarded the contract for which the famous 'A' Shop was amended for its new role.

New locomotive building returned to Swindon in BREL days when in 1980 a fleet of 20 metre gauge 0-8-0 diesel hydraulic shunting locomotives were constructed for Kenya Railways, the locomotives being completed to an operational condition and then packed for despatch by sea to Africa.

Although Swindon's 'A' Shop had not reverberated to the sound of a 'King' or 'Castle' under repair for many years, steam traction still visited the Works occasionally, either in the form of one of the three Vale of Rheidol narrow gauge locomotives, or a privately owned example being repaired under contract.

In the mid-1980s, prior to the announcement of closure,

the main locomotive activity at Swindon was the general overhaul and installation of dual brake equipment on Class 08s; with on average one locomotive being completed each week during 1984 and 1985.

For well over the last decade, prior to closure, Swindon Works had a department solely engaged on scrapping redundant equipment. This included locomotives, coaches, wagons and plant, with sizeable yards at the country end of the Works becoming the graveyard for many locomotives. In addition to scrapping locomotives, Swindon provided accommodation for the storage of locomotives whilst decisions were made on their future.

In addition to dealing with locomotives and rolling stock, Swindon also dealt with CCE overhauls for a number of years, including repairs to cranes, tampers and ballast machines.

A sizeable non-ferrous foundry was provided at Swindon supplying BREL, BR and the private sector with castings. One of the major undertakings of this plant in more recent years was the casting and preparation of locomotive nameplates.

In the summer of 1985 BREL announced that the Swindon Works would be closed with effect from mid-1986. This came as a bombshell to the employees, but as BREL justified at the time of the announcement, declining order books and the lack of contracts from its main customer (BR) meant that work practices had to be rationalised and this regrettably led to the closure of the Works.

In the mid-1970s the following main Shops could be found at Swindon:

Diesel Erecting Shop This was once the famous Swindon 'A' shop and undertook the building, repair and modifications to all locomotives visiting the Works. In recent years this was mainly confined to Class 08s, but a handful of Classes 27, 31, 37 and 47 did make visits for minor repairs – usually to collision damage. It was in this area that the SR CEP/BEP refurbishing programme was carried out and most locomotives were stripped prior to cutting.

Civil Engineering Department Again this occupied part of the old 'A' shop and carried out repairs to CCE road and rail equipment.

Copper & Sheet Metal Shop Pipework and sheet metal components were formed and repaired here, and welding of large aluminium structures was possible. Overhead cranes were provided for easy movement. The repair of lamps was also effected in this area.

Machine Shop Most new components were manufactured in this Shop and many items for repair work fabricated. The usual range of electronically controlled machines was installed.

Diesel Test House All diesel engines or completed locomotives passed through here for final testing prior to release into traffic. Adjacent was the famous Swindon Works turntable which remained hand operated until the Works finally closed.

Pattern Shop This Shop produced all the necessary patterns and castings for use in the Works foundry.

Engine Shop It was within this Shop that all types of diesel engine were repaired. Fuel injectors and other delicate items were repaired in an adjoining Shop, as were propshafts for which special balancing equipment was installed.

Non-Ferrous Foundry Large castings were produced in this Shop, about 50% of its output going to the private sector. The Foundry had the responsibility of casting many locomotive nameplates.

Bogie & Wheel Shop In this Shop wheels, tyres and axles were machined and assembled. Fabricated bogies were also assembled here. A section of this Shop was devoted to repairing existing bogies from both loco-hauled and dmu vehicles.

Carriage Repair Shop This section carried out repairs to NPCCS vehicles in addition to dmu stock. Lifting jacks were provided enabling vehicle bodies to be raised clear of wheelsets, which were then despatched to the relevant repair shop. Special sections were dedicated to woodwork, panelling, upholstery, doors, windows and pipework. Another special section was devoted to painting and detail completion.

Brake Equipment Shop Situated adjacent to the Non-Ferrous Foundry, this Department undertook repairs to air compressors, vacuum exhausters and all types of brake control equipment. Rolling stock brake cylinders were also repaired here.

Wagon Shop This sizeable section of the complex carried out the overhaul and repair to all types of wagon. Adjoining was a sawmill for the preparation of timber used in repair work.

Smiths' Shop A vast number of components from both carriages and wagons were repaired here. Flash butt-welding, steam hammer work and a multitude of iron operations were carried out.

Spring Shop As indicated by its name this Shop's main activity was the manufacture and repair of all types of railway used spring.

Test House This facility produced all types of lifting sling for both Works and outside use. Special test facilities were installed to meet stringent factory standards and requirements governed by the Safe Working Loads (SWL).

Several stores and ancillary shops were provided around the Works, including a Weigh Shop where all locomotives passed before returning to traffic, and an Asbestos Removal Plant which, in more recent years, was used to remove this potentially dangerous substance from a number of railway vehicles.

A sizeable Works Training School, constructed in 1962, was located on the opposite side of the main line to the Works, and could accommodate 112 apprentices. The building was equipped with all modern machinery, a lecture room and laboratory area. Apprentices usually spent one year at the school before taking up employment at the main Works. A large Staff Canteen with the usual social facilities was provided for the Works staff.

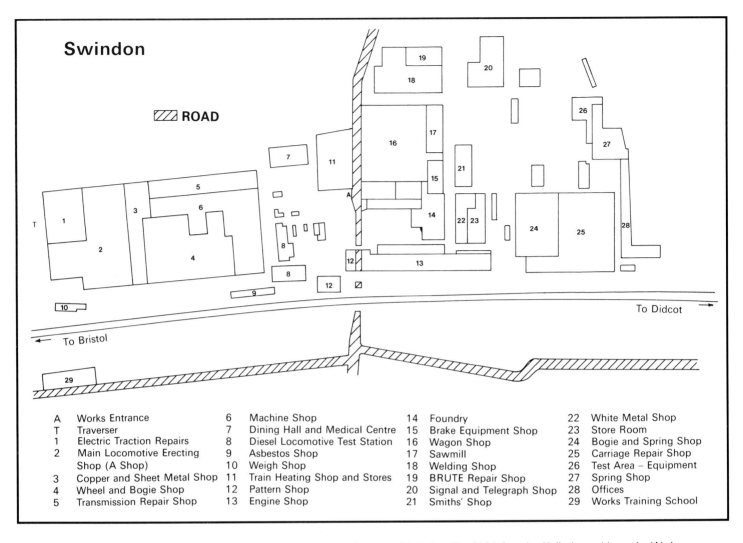

Swindon

▨ **ROAD**

A	Works Entrance	6	Machine Shop	14	Foundry	22	White Metal Shop
T	Traverser	7	Dining Hall and Medical Centre	15	Brake Equipment Shop	23	Store Room
1	Electric Traction Repairs	8	Diesel Locomotive Test Station	16	Wagon Shop	24	Bogie and Spring Shop
2	Main Locomotive Erecting	9	Asbestos Shop	17	Sawmill	25	Carriage Repair Shop
	Shop (A Shop)	10	Weigh Shop	18	Welding Shop	26	Test Area – Equipment
3	Copper and Sheet Metal Shop	11	Train Heating Shop and Stores	19	BRUTE Repair Shop	27	Spring Shop
4	Wheel and Bogie Shop	12	Pattern Shop	20	Signal and Telegraph Shop	28	Offices
5	Transmission Repair Shop	13	Engine Shop	21	Smiths' Shop	29	Works Training School

In the days when steam still reigned supreme at Swindon, 'Hall' class No. 6924 *Grantley Hall* takes a ride on the 'A' shop traverser, while two 'Western' class Type 4 diesel hydraulics are seen in the repair bays.

J. Patel

When the locomotives arrived 'on Works' for major overhauls the first job after the initial inspection was de-fuelling, after which locomotives passed on to the Stripping Shop or Repair bay depending on the nature of overhaul. Virtually all items, ranging from the driver's seat to the power unit, were removed. This illustration shows the Stripping Shop at Swindon in BR Workshop days, housing NBL Type 2 No. D6311 and 'Modified Hall' No. 7912 *Little Linford Hall*.

J. Patel

Following agreement between the Germany licence holders and the BTC for the construction of diesel hydraulics in the UK, Swindon Workshops were awarded a constructional contract for 38 B-B locomotives, in later years to become the D800 or 'Warship' class. Two early members of the build are seen in the 'A' Shop in company with 'Castle' class No. 5024 *Carew Castle*.

J. Patel

With the demise of steam traction Swindon's main workload was the repair of diesel hydraulic traction. Type 3 'Hymek' No. D7009 poses alongside maroon liveried Type 4 'Warship' No. D805 *Benbow*. The large amount of cable present around the cab end suggests that the 'Hymek', was being rewired.

Colin J. Marsden

When the number of traction units operated by BR is taken into account, and the number of miles each travels per year, the frequency of accidents is few. Regrettably, by nature of the transport system operated, when accidents do occur the results are often catastrophic. Thankfully the skill and expertise of workshop staff usually rectifies damage with little or no trace. Class 52 No. D1049 *Western Monarch* poses in the Works yard awaiting assessment after severe collision damage in 1969.

Colin J. Marsden

Another Swindon masterpiece! The final diesel hydraulic ever to receive classified attention at Swindon was Class 52 'Western' No. D1023 *Western Fusilier*, which was returned to traffic in September 1973. The locomotive is seen here in immaculate condition outside Swindon Works prior to operating its recommissioning test train.

After an absence of 18 years, diesel hydraulic locomotive building returned to the Works in 1980, when a fleet of 20 0-8-0 diesel hydraulic shunting locomotives was constructed for the metre gauge Kenya Railways under sub-contract to Hunslet of Leeds. Locomotive No. 4716 stands inside the Works prior to despatch to Africa via road and sea.

Over the years the expertise of the Swindon workforce brought additional revenue to the Company by repairing and restoring some withdrawn steam locomotives. LMS No. 6229 *Duchess of Hamilton* was rebuilt at the Works during 1975-76 and parts of the tender and cab are seen here in November 1975 prior to reassembly.

Brian Morrison

The testing of diesel locomotive power units is an important operation at any works, and Swindon, in common with the majority of establishments, had a sizeable Test House where complete locomotives, or just power units, could be put through their paces. This view shows the inside of the soundproofed control room, while a Maybach power unit is operated under load control conditions in the test area.

In the late 1970s new, rather obstrusive, roller shutter doors and a coach length vehicle traverser, were installed at the west end of the Main Shop, to assist with the then current SR emu refurbishing programme. Class 411 TS No. S70666, to be fitted in unit 1608, is illustrated on the traverser outside No. 23 road.

J. Patel

Class 411 refurbishing in full swing. The contract for the complete rebuilding of nearly 500 SR emu cars was a major boost to the dwindling Swindon order books of the late 1970s and early 1980s. In this view, taken in the spring of 1980, four vehicles can be seen awaiting refitting.

Colin J. Marsden

Two test engineers observe the operation of a power unit inside the Swindon Test Centre. Note that both men are wearing special ear protection.

The work involved in the Class 411/412 refurbishing scheme consisted of complete internal stripping, fitting new windows, altering the internal coach layouts to put the guard's accommodation in the middle of the unit, rebogieing, and then rebuilding with the latest style of seats and decor. Three cars are seen in the advanced stage of repair in this view taken in the autumn of 1980.

Colin J. Marsden

With increasing awareness of possible health hazards involving asbestos insulation in recent years, the railways have undertaken a major project of asbestos removal. To conform with very strict Health & Safety Regulations, all staff involved in removal work must wear 'space style' clothing with oxygen purifying masks. The Asbestos Removal Shop was almost air-tight to ensure that no asbestos dust escaped into the atmosphere. Two of Swindon's asbestos team are seen here surveying the front of a dmu.

A number of dmus, mainly those allocated to the London Midland and Western Regions, were looked after by the Works. Here, a driving car of a Class 116 unit is supported on four high-capacity screw jacks during repair work. The missing front end panels suggest that the car had either received collision damage or was having corroded panels replaced.

A Cardiff Division Class 120 DMS stands supported on the electronically operated screw jacks of the DMU Shop during classified attention in March 1979. When lifting or lowering the vehicles, all four jacks would be synchronised to ensure that the vehicle is moved on the perfect true.

Graham Scott-Lowe

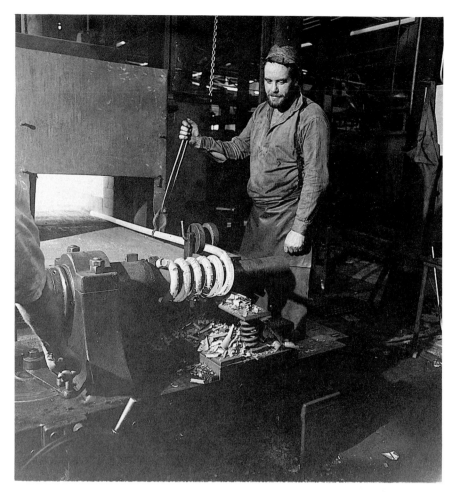

In addition to locomotive and rolling stock repairs, Swindon Works was equipped as a full engineering factory, able to undertake virtually any requirement for the railway or private sector. This picture shows the Spring Shop with a white hot rod of steel emerging from a furnace being formed into a coil spring.

One Department within the Works dealt with the maintenance and heavy repair of Civil Engineering mechanical plant, including such items as CCE locomotives, ballast cleaning machines, tampers, liners and cranes. A crane base is seen in this illustration in 1977.

From the early 1970s, until the closure of the Works in 1986, Swindon was one of the country's major diesel graveyards, cutting up literally hundreds of locomotives. In this view of the Works' scrapyard in 1977 no fewer than eight 'Western' Class 52s can be seen awaiting their call to the cutter's torch. The locomotive nearest the camera is No. D1012 (*Western Firebrand*).
Colin J. Marsden

The only non-ferrous foundry within the BREL Group was located at Swindon, producing castings of all sizes for both BR and the private sector. A 2¹/₂ cwt capacity hoist is seen being filled with molten metal from one of the furnaces.
Colin J. Marsden

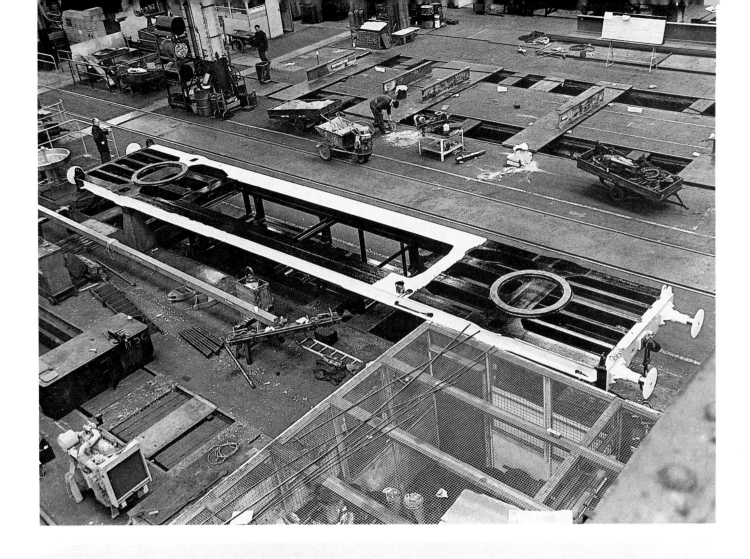

Temple Mills

The only London based BREL establishment was at Temple Mills, near Stratford in East London. In 1847 the 'Railway King' – George Hudson – decided to build his workshop facilities for the Eastern Counties Railway (ECR) at Stratford, this later becoming the basis for the Great Eastern Railway (GER). In the closing years of the 19th century expansion of the Stratford complex was such that additional facilities were required. Suitable land was found about one mile away at Temple Mills, and a wagon construction and repair facility was founded.

Temple Mills and Stratford operated alongside one another until 1963, when the BR Workshops Division closed Stratford Locomotive Works, but retained the Temple Mills unit, although largely altered and updated, mainly to accommodate modern freight vehicles, some of which were operated in 'block' formations such as Freightliner or Cartics. At the same time a Bogie Repair Plant was commissioned and a number of new sophisticated machines installed, including two additional overhead cranes. Temple Mills Works became the major repair point in the mid/late 1960s for the rapidly expanding Freightliner and automotive fleets, which regularly operated to and from nearby railheads such as the London International Freight Terminal or the Ford Motor Car Plant at Dagenham.

When BREL was formed in January 1970 Temple Mills was absorbed into the group structure, mass rebuilding and modernisation followed which included the redevelopment of the container repair activity enabling the most modern, all-metal ISO containers for BR and private enterprise to be repaired. During 1974 a shot-blasting facility was installed to meet refurbishing requirements for container and 'Presflo' wagons. Further alterations to the Works came in 1975-77 when a flowline for refurbishing containers and bulk wagons was introduced.

An amount of 'special pioneering' work was undertaken in the 1960-70s when various 'mock-ups' for Freightliner and automotive stock were produced. Some support work for the original Channel Tunnel project was also carried out at the Works, mainly involving new high speed wagon designs.

In addition to railway wagon maintenance the Works had responsibility for a considerable number of BR road vehicles and their associated trailers.

During the late 1970s the Works employed some 400 staff and occupied a site of approximately 22 acres, six acres of which were covered buildings. In 1982 the BREL Group decided to rationalize their wagon undertaking and close the smallest of their operations at Temple Mills with effect from the end of 1983. All work after closure was transferred to Doncaster.

In the period immediately prior to closure the Works was formed of the following Departments:

Presflo & Bogie Repair Shop Repairs to Pressure Flow (Presflo) and bogie vehicles were carried out in this 2-track Shop where overhead crane and jacking equipment was provided.

Welding & Press Shop This Shop had four main activities: one section was fitted with six electric welding booths for component and item repairs, another section dealt with the overhaul of vacuum and air brake cylinders which also incorporated sophisticated test equipment. A further section of the Shop housed hydraulic presses and furnaces for component repair to such items as axle guards and straightening of wagon sides. The fourth section covered the general fitting facility for the overhaul of wheelsets and roller bearing axle boxes.

Container Shops Nos 1 & 2 Two large container facilities were located at this Works – Shop 1 – the larger of the two – was the original Freightliner Container point, having facilities for practically any repair. In addition to BR containers a number of privately owned containers were also maintained. Shop 2 opened in 1977, catered for the additional demand generated by the rapid expansion of the containerized freight network.

Shot Blast Shop Formed in the 1977 Works reorganisation, this Shot Blast facility was used to remove all waste particles from wagon bodies prior to repair. The shot was reclaimed for further use.

Paint Shop Significant rebuilding of this Shop was carried out in 1976, the main feature being the modern paint spray booth which operated on negative pressure, low level extraction meeting the latest safety requirements being installed. All general overhaul vehicles and containers were passed through this Shop before returning to service.

Wood Machining Shop This was equipped with the usual wood preparation tools and machines to make timber ready for wagon and container repairs.

Machine Shop This facility undertook turning, milling, drilling, planing and slotting operations. A number of special wagon components were manufactured here for Works and outside use. A Works Maintenance Department was provided in one section of the Shop.

Smithy Shop Most metal components for wagon and container building/repair were dealt with here. Flash-butt welding equipment and laminated spring test facilities were installed, as were two steam-powered hammers.

Wagon Body Repair Shop This 3-road Shop was dedicated to the overhaul of all non-bogie freight stock, each line being fully equipped for all body and underframe repairs.

Cartic & Freightliner Repair Shop All Freightliner and automotive wagons were repaired in this area. Two roads were provided together with an amount of side preparation space. A section of the Shop was dedicated to bogie repairs. Internal movement was by overhead gantry crane.

Wagon Lifting Shop All non-bogie vehicles visiting the Works for classified attention were taken through this Shop on a progressive flowline system, with vehicle lifting carried out by overhead crane. Special facilities existed for underframe overhauls, ultra-sonic axle testing and wheel turning.

To ease vehicle movement around the Works three wagon traversers linking together the main Shops were provided. In addition to the Shops detailed above there were a small number of ancillary sections covering fibreglass, general fitting and detail painting. A small Medical Centre, a fully equipped Canteen and Staff Welfare facilities were also provided.

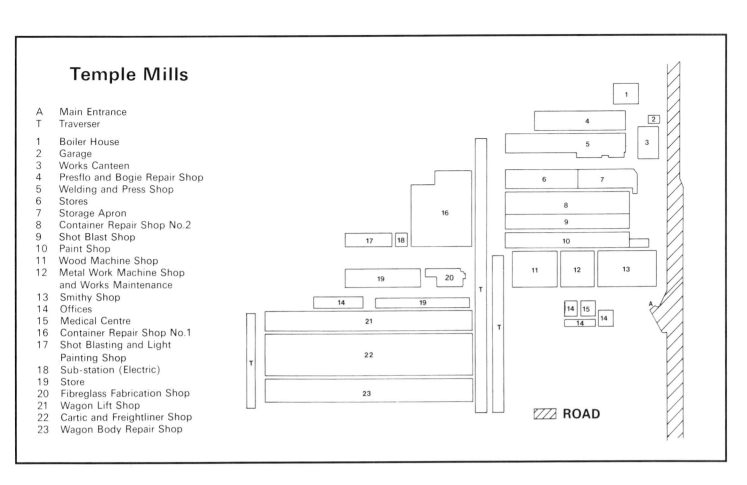

Temple Mills

A   Main Entrance
T   Traverser

1   Boiler House
2   Garage
3   Works Canteen
4   Presflo and Bogie Repair Shop
5   Welding and Press Shop
6   Stores
7   Storage Apron
8   Container Repair Shop No.2
9   Shot Blast Shop
10 Paint Shop
11 Wood Machine Shop
12 Metal Work Machine Shop
    and Works Maintenance
13 Smithy Shop
14 Offices
15 Medical Centre
16 Container Repair Shop No.1
17 Shot Blasting and Light
    Painting Shop
18 Sub-station (Electric)
19 Store
20 Fibreglass Fabrication Shop
21 Wagon Lift Shop
22 Cartic and Freightliner Shop
23 Wagon Body Repair Shop

ROAD

A view taken inside the main Vehicle Repair Shop showing a 12 ton box van, a 16 ton mineral wagon, two 'Presflo' wagons and a grain hopper under repair. In the roof, a 15 ton crane is provided, capable of lifting most vehicles clear of their wheelsets.

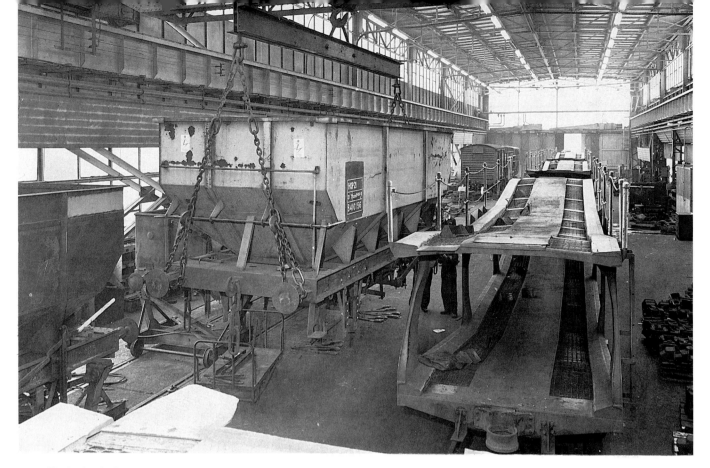

The body of a 21 ton coal hopper is seen being lifted clear of its wheels in preparation for transfer from one section of the Works to another. In the foreground a privately owned 'Cartic 4' set is seen under repair. Note the special swivel intermediate coupling visible on the near end, connecting the vehicle over the articulated bogie.

Colin J. Marsden

The side stepboards of a goods brakevan are seen being replaced by a Works' 'chippy', while on the right, a metal bodied open wagon, a box van, and various open vehicles are receiving attention in the Wagon Shop. For safety reasons, all equipment and repair stores in use are kept well out of the way towards the centre of the Shop.

Under the precise control of two cranes, each being guided by a separate member of floor staff, a Tunnel Bulk Cement 'Presflo' wagon is lifted clear of its wheels in May 1975. Note that a fitter is holding each axle head to prevent the wheels rolling away. All staff involved in the lifting procedure are wearing statutory head protection.

Colin J. Marsden

On completion of vehicle repairs, and prior to the stock being returned to its owners or relevant BR operating department, a stringent test programme was effected, covering all operational parts, with a special emphasis being placed on brakes. The 'Cartic 4' illustrated has shore supply air connections attached during a brake test.

Wolverton

BREL Wolverton Works was located on the northern boundaries of Milton Keynes, mid-way between Euston and Birmingham. The Works' history can be traced back to 1838 when the London & Birmingham Railway (L&BR) erected their locomotive workshops adjacent to Wolverton station. The workshops, occupied just two acres and employed around 100 staff, and continued building and maintaining locomotives until 1865 when the L&BR was absorbed by the London & Northern Western Railway Company (LNWR). The directors of this company soon decreed that all locomotive construction would in future be carried out at Crewe, while Wolverton would continue and become the Company's major carriage and wagon works. Over the ensuing years Wolverton Works gradually expanded but still remained solely responsible for carriage and wagon stock. From 1923 the Works was taken over by the LMS which continued its existence as the Company's main carriage and wagon operation.

After Nationalisation in 1948 the Works was retained by the BTC as a major carriage and wagon unit, and during the following years it built many hundreds of new passenger coaches as replacements for old pre-Nationalisation stock.

Following publication of the BTC Modernisation Plan, Wolverton was given the brief to construct some emu stock as well as loco-hauled vehicles.

Details of the Wolverton traction construction programme:

Class	Formation	Total	Years
304	BDTS, MBS, TC		
	DTBS	45	1960-61
504	DMBS, DTS	25	1959-60

By 1962 the BTC/BR Workshops Division deemed that Wolverton should be solely responsible for repair work, placing all subsequent constructional contracts with other Works. From the 1960s Wolverton carried out classified, casual and collision repairs to most ER and LMR emus together with a large number of loco-hauled vehicles.

From January 1970 Wolverton Works was operated by BREL and in the months that followed considerable reorganisation and re-equipment took place. Then, from the late 1970s, when refurbishing of 'old' stock was in vogue, Wolverton played a major role; by 1985 several hundred ER units including most members of Classes 307, 308 and 309, had passed through the Works. In most cases their major rebuilding meant the opening out of compartment vehicles, installation of lower false ceilings, public address systems, and modern decor, as well as updated technical equipment. During mid-1985 some SR Class 422 (4BIG) units also passed through the Works for refurbishing.

On the hauled vehicle front, Wolverton constructed a large number of MK I coaches of the BSK, BSO, CK, FO, RMB, SK, SLC, SLF, SLS and BG types, as well as Post Office vehicles.

From Spring 1986, when BREL was altered to form two separate divisions, the Company relinquished responsibility for Wolverton, handing the site over to British Rail Maintenance Ltd (BRML), who have continued site operation at its previous level, but with the addition of IC125 trailer vehicle repairs.

The present Wolverton site, now deemed as one of the most important Carriage Centres in Europe, occupies a site of 73 acres and employs well over 1,000 staff.

During 1985 the BREL Works was formed of the following Shops:

Wheel Shop All repairs to wheels were carried out in this area including turning, re-tyring, re-axling and ultra-sonic axle testing. Other services included the overhaul to disc brake equipment and roller bearing axle boxes.

Initial Inspection Shop This section, adjacent to the Wheel Shop, was where all loco-hauled vehicles were examined for defects before passing to the main Repair Shops. Items tested included heating and water systems and lighting units. Many interior components were removed from vehicles whilst in this area.

Lifting Shop Carriage bodies were lifted off their bogies here by overhead cranes, with vehicle bogies being cleaned, stripped and then repaired, while coach underframes, draw gear, heating and brake systems were overhauled.

Carriage Repair Shop Three large Shops came under this collective title. 1. Refurbishing Repair Shop. 2. Coach Repair Shop West. 3. Coach Repair Shop East. The Refurbishing Repair Shop undertook all major rebuilding and refurbishment which could not readily be undertaken in the normal repair bays. The Coach Repair Shop West and East were progressive flowline repair areas where all interior fittings were removed, bodies repaired if necessary and then progressively refitted. The West Shop had a large press and metal guillotine for the manufacture of body panels.

Trimming Shop Adjacent to Coach Repair Shop East was the Trimming Shop which undertook all upholstery repairs including curtains.

Sawmill The Sawmill formed part of the Production Services Group of the Works and housed a variety of machines and equipment to manufacture timber products used for coach repairs.

Smiths' Shop All blacksmiths' work was undertaken here for use within the Works. This included a section dealing with the repair of laminated springs.

Paint Shop All completed vehicles passed through here for cosmetic attention, paint being normally applied by the brush technique. Adjoining the Paint Shop was a high voltage test and final inspection area.

Traction Shop This section overhauled all traction motors, electric control compartments and emu power bogies. Unit power cars were usually taken into the Shop and jacked clear of their bogies for removal and repair.

Machine, Fitting & Welding Shop This group of Shops was installed with modern electronic machines to manufacture and repair most metal components required for vehicles visiting the Works. The Shops also carried out electric welding and oxy-gas cutting. A section of the Shop catered for maintenance of works plant including the manufacture of jigs.

Electric Repair Shop Here the manufacture and repair of train lighting equipment, including dynamos, regulators, controllers and couplings was effected. All electric auxiliary machines were dealt with in this area.

Cell Shop Lead acid batteries were manufactured in this Shop and charged in an adjacent section. Batteries were supplied to all parts of the railway and mainly used for carriage lighting.

Brass Shop All metal fittings on vehicles were repaired in this area, including door handles, locks, steam and air valves, toilet and water equipment. Facilities existed for electro-plating of copper, nickel, chrome, cadmium and zinc.

Works Training School This was situated just outside the main Works complex, able to accommodate 72 craft apprentices for a one year off-the-job training course. An additional apprentice training area was located within the East Coach Repair Shop.

In addition to the Shops detailed above, other smaller sections of the Works included a Tin Shop, Millwrights' Shop, Polishing Shop, Plastics Shop, Asbestos Removal Shop and Timber Store. There were also a number of equipment stores located around the Works as well as the usual Office and Management units. A Staff Canteen was situated adjacent to the Works entrance, together with a small Fire Station.

Wolverton has for many years been responsible for storage and maintenance of the Royal Train stock, this in recent years having included the rebuilding of a number of Mk III vehicles for Royal Train use.

Wolverton

A	Main Entrance	
T	Traverser	
1	Offices	
2	Welding Shop	
3	Machine and Fitting Shop	
4	Stores	
5	Millwrights' Shop	
6	Cell Charging Shop	
7	Electric Repair Shop	
8	Cell Shop	
9	Tin Shop	
10	Brass Shop	
11	Works Canteen	
12	Plastics Shop	
13	Works Maintenance	
14	Medical Centre	
15	Traction Shop	
16	Works Training School	
17	Paint Shop	
18	Final Inspection Shop	
19	High Voltage Test Shop	
20	Smiths' Shop	
21	Polishing Shop	
22	Sawmill	
23	Boiler House	
24	Coach Repair Shop East	
25	Works Training School	
26	Trimming Shop	
27	Coach Repair Shop West	
28	Press Shop	
29	Refurbish and Heavy Repair Shop	
30	First Aid Point	
31	Lifting Shop	
32	Asbestos Shop	
33	Timber Shop	
34	Wheel Shop	
35	Initial Examination Shop	

In more recent years one of the main briefs given to Wolverton was the classified overhaul of loco-hauled and emu vehicles, with loco-hauled stock from Western, Eastern and London Midland Regions being the most frequent visitors. Two overhead cranes slowly lift Mk IIf FO No. W3396 in readiness for bogie refitting.

Virtually the entire ER emu fleet has received attention at Wolverton, latterly with most classes receiving heavy refurbishment. Class 305/2 Battery Driving Trailer Second (BDTS) No. E75433 of unit No. 305510 is supported by two 25 ton overhead cranes during bogie replacement in early 1980. In the foreground one of the vehicle's bogies with the AWS receiver in front is seen.

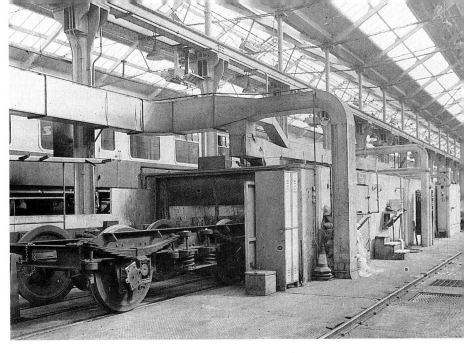

In addition to vehicle repairs a major portion of the Works' activities involved the maintenance of component parts, such as bogies, brake equipment etc. A purpose-built CERA bogie washing plant was installed at Wolverton and used to wash bogies before repairs were effected. A rather decrepit looking B1 bogie is seen by the plant in this illustration.

Taylor Alden Ltd

Only two Workshops within the BREL Group undertook repairs to Royal Mail 'Travelling Post Office' stock – Wolverton and York. In 1976-77 24 new TPO vehicles were taken into stock, all being Wolverton rebuilds of SK vehicles. Post Office Sorting Van No. W80390 is seen in the advanced stages of conversion in this 20th January 1977 illustration. This vehicle was formerly SK No. 25047.

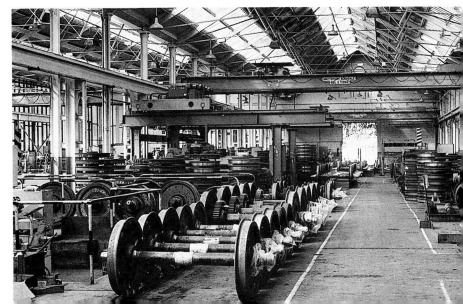

The large Wolverton Wheel Shop was equipped not only to produce wheels and bogies for repaired rolling stock, but also to fulfil regional requirements. This had facilities to turn, re-tyre and re-axle as necessary. Ultra-sonic test equipment was also provided. This illustration gives a general view of the Shop.

Colin J. Marsden

Looking more as if it is suffering from an incurable disease, Class 507 TS No. M71361 stands parted from its driving cars during a classified overhaul. The spots are areas of bodywork where undercoat has been applied to ensure a good finished paint surface. Note the special coupling converter enabling the bar coupling to be connected to conventional locomotive couplings.

Colin J. Marsden

Following the completion of repairs to coaching and unit vehicles a stringent test programme followed. This being particularly relevant to emu stock where, on most units complicated electronic circuitry is found. Class 313 No. 313052 is seen inside the high voltage Test House.

Colin J. Marsden

One of the major undertakings at Wolverton in recent years was emu refurbishment. This work consisted of gutting each vehicle down to the basic metal shell and completely rebuilding. In many cases this included the opening out of compartment vehicles, fitting internal gangways, and in some cases, altering the position of the guard's accommodation. The DTS of Class 305 No. 305410 stands on Matterson jacks in the Main Shop in May 1985.

Michael J. Collins

Pantograph Motor Second (PMS) No. M62707 from Class 317 No. 317347, stands separated from its set inside one of the repair shops during March 1985. Note that the equipment in front of the coach is mounted on a pallet to facilitate easy transfer around the Works.

Michael J. Collins

The first refurbished Class 309 "Essex Express" emerged from Wolverton in Spring 1985, painted in the then London & South East "Jaffacake" livery. During refurbishment work the front ends were not greatly altered except for the installation of a sealed beam headlight. The first refurbished Class 309, No. 309605 was photographed in March 1985 nearing completion.

Michael J. Collins

This view, also of the Class 309 refurbishing, shows the vehicle in a far more advanced state than the previous illustration, with the floor, hopper windows and roof insulation, as well as the first body partition, in position.

Michael J. Collins

Although the refurbishing programme was underway, due to limitations of finance and workshop space, not all units could be refurbished. This illustration shows a Class 302 TC vehicle, No. E70206 undergoing an intermediate overhaul in the Carriage Repair Shop.

Colin J. Marsden

▼

As with all Works establishments, staff safety was one of the most important factors surrounding each activity. The two men in this illustration cutting away part of a vehicle's bodywork during refurbishment, are wearing BR-supplied ear, face and inhalation protection. The man using the angle grinder is also wearing a protective glove.

◄

During refurbishment, after vehicle bodies were gutted and new window openings made if required, one of the first refitting jobs was the sound-proofing and draught-proofing of the floors. This operation is seen in progress in a Class 309 vehicle.

Michael J. Collins

With its bodywork in part primer, Newspaper van No. 95323 stands in the paintshop when this January 1988 view was taken. This coach was a rebuild from a standard BG by the removal of guards facilities.

Michael J. Collins

For many years the British Royal Train has been stabled in sidings adjacent to Wolverton Works when not in use. Although we are unable to include illustrations inside the Royal Train shed, we are able to show two now-withdrawn Royal Sleeping Cars posed in the Works yard.

Colin J. Marsden

With modern emu types now in service the period between classified overhauls is considerably extended to that of the older style stock, with the average 1972 derivative high-density unit only visiting the plant every 4-5 years for attention. Class 313 Motor Second (MS) No. E62647 is seen outside the test bay in this 1985 illustration.

Colin J. Marsden

Painted in the distinctive orange and brown livery of Greater Manchester PTE, Class 303 MBS No. M61833 of set No. 303057 is pulled onto one of the traversers in January 1988 after receiving classified attention.

Michael J. Collins

York

The BREL establishment at York – located to the north east of the city – was the former York Carriage Works built by the North Eastern Railway (NER) in 1884. The workshops were never designed for locomotive activity and indeed have remained dedicated to coach work ever since. Between 1884 and the Grouping in 1923 the Works rapidly expanded with the construction of a number of new Shops. Between Grouping and Nationalisation the Works remained in control of the LNER coach fleets and additionally constructed a number of new vehicles.

From 1st January 1948 when the Works came under the BTC, later BR, flag, the first major task set was the repair of many hundreds of war damaged items, but by 1951 things had considerably changed. After four years of national control, and having taken check on all stock acquired under Nationalisation, the BTC decided to opt for a standard coaching stock type, and thus the Mk I was born. Like many of the BR workshops, York was heavily involved in this project, which continued the Work's association with coach building. Towards the end of the 1950s a considerable number of emu sets were authorised, with a number constructed at York. Over the ensuing years the Works has become the nation's established emu builder, this continuing right to the sell-off of the BREL Company. A £1 million investment was placed in the Works during the mid-1960s for extensive reorganisation and modernisation, including the rebuilding of many Shops and installation of latest machines and equipment. A centralised Stores was also provided, together with a number of new sidings for vehicle storage.

After 1st January 1970 when the Works came under the BREL flag, the main brief of the plant was the continuation of coach repairs and construction of new multiple unit stock.

York Works electric multiple unit build:

Class	Total (Vehicles)	Years
302	448*	1959-60
305	165	1960-61
305	76	1960
308	180	1961
309	76	1962-63
312	196	1975-77
313	192	1976-77
314	48	1979
315	244	1980
317	216	1982-87
318	63	1986
319	240	1987-88
321	284	1988-89
420	112	1965-70
421	552	1964-70
423	776	1967-75
430	60+	1966-74
455	505	1983-85
491	132++	1966-74
507	120	1978-79
508	172	1979-80

*Frames only.
+30 cars rebuilt from loco-hauled stock.
++All rebuilt from loco-hauled stock.

York Works diesel multiple unit build:

Class	Total (Sets)	Years
150	278*	1984-87

*Includes two departmental vehicles.

Following the formation of BREL it was within the brief of the Company to tender for overseas contracts, and throughout the 1970s various contracts for overseas administrations were fulfilled. This included work for Northern Ireland Railways and the production of electric InterCity units for Taiwan.

The York Repair Shops, under BREL, had capacity for renovation and repair to vehicles at the rate of approximately 50 per week. Coaches of virtually any type were able to be accommodated, as well as passenger stock, NPCCS and special purpose vehicles were regularly seen.

In 1983-84 York constructed two prototype dmu sets classified 150 – these were the first diesel vehicles constructed by the Works. Following successful tests a production run of 272 2-car Class 150 sets were constructed, being introduced between 1984 and 1987.

As well as its new build role, York Works had played a major part in maintenance and repair work on emu fleets, in recent years this being confined mainly to post 1972 design high density types.

The main Shops at the BREL Works at the time of the 'sell off' were as follows:

Lift Shop When vehicles arrived at the Works they passed through this Shop, bodies being lifted off their bogies, to enable inspection and repair; including attention to underframes, heating and brake gear. Wheel lathes were installed, together with ultra-sonic flaw detection equipment.

Frame Shop Adjoining the Lift Shop, this facility dealt with the construction of new underframes, together with an amount of bogie work. The various frame assemblies being welded in jigs and then passed to the New Build Shop for completion.

Repair Shop After vehicles passed through the Lift Shop, and mounted on accommodation bogies, they were taken to the Repair Shop where all interior and body repairs were effected; this work included most refitting.

Electric Shop This Shop had the responsibility to overhaul all electrical components from both loco-hauled and multiple unit stock.

Plumbers' Shop Repairs to metal fittings including door locks were carried out here, as was some repairs to pipework for water and gas equipment.

Machine Shop All milling, drilling, turning, slotting and grinding operations were carried out in this area. Adjacent to the Shop was a Works Tool Room where jigs and tools were assembled.

New Build Shop The New Build Shop was operated on a flowline principle. Vehicle shells being brought into the Shop at one end and progressively constructed to emerge at the other as complete vehicles, which then passed to the Paint Shop.

Paint Shop This received all new and most repaired vehicles for external preparation and painting before return to traffic. Special spray booths were provided for stove enamelling and detail finishing.

Trimming Shop This facility handled all coach upholstery, including seats, curtains and floor coverings. Special equipment included modern sewing machines.

Press Shop All metal pressings were prepared from raw products in this section, where large guillotines and numerous presses were provided. A phosphating plant was used for anti-corrosive treatment of new products.

Saw Mill The Saw Mill was equipped as a high capacity wood preparation area, and as well as supplying the Works with materials, it also supplied the BR Regions with wooden components for vehicle repair. A notable feature was the sawdust extraction system connected to the Works incinerator, where burning of waste chippings assisted in providing power for Works services.

Test Centre As part of the continued quality assurance of Works products, a Test Centre was provided, where all completed stock was tested prior to despatch.

In addition to the Shops mentioned above the following were also provided to give support facilities: Fabrication Shop, Smith Shop, Battery Shop, Component Wash Shop, Flame-cutters' Shop, Wheel Shop and Container Repair Shop. Three full sized traversers were provided adjacent to the Main Building to give access between Shops and the different facilities. Several office buildings existed around the Works, looking after the day to day functions. There was also a Staff Canteen near the main Works Entrance as well as a fully equipped Training School.

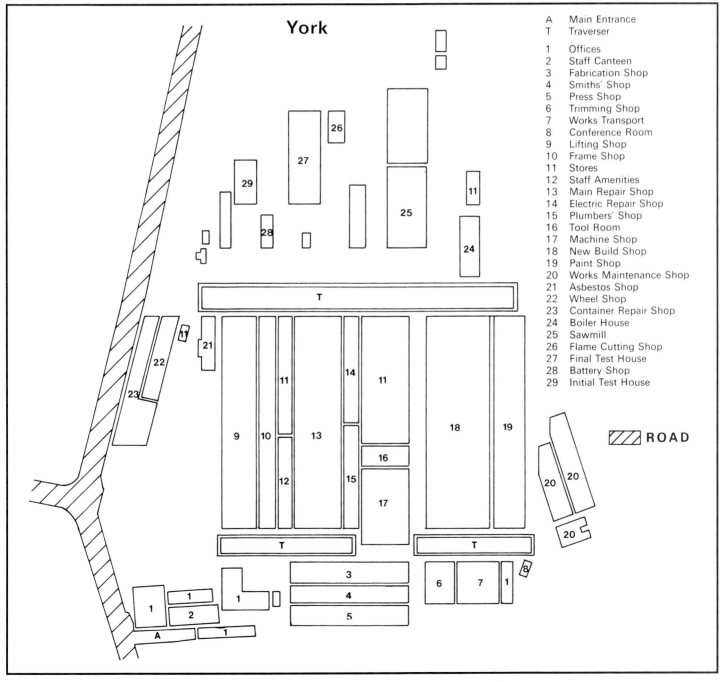

York

A	Main Entrance
T	Traverser
1	Offices
2	Staff Canteen
3	Fabrication Shop
4	Smiths' Shop
5	Press Shop
6	Trimming Shop
7	Works Transport
8	Conference Room
9	Lifting Shop
10	Frame Shop
11	Stores
12	Staff Amenities
13	Main Repair Shop
14	Electric Repair Shop
15	Plumbers' Shop
16	Tool Room
17	Machine Shop
18	New Build Shop
19	Paint Shop
20	Works Maintenance Shop
21	Asbestos Shop
22	Wheel Shop
23	Container Repair Shop
24	Boiler House
25	Sawmill
26	Flame Cutting Shop
27	Final Test House
28	Battery Shop
29	Initial Test House

ROAD

A general view of the Frame Shop, with the Lifting Shop being adjacent. This Shop dealt with the fabrication of vehicle underframes, as well as a small amount of bogie work. A number of rotary welding jigs were used in this area and are clearly visible in the illustration.

Between 1975 and 1977 BREL York constructed a fleet of 49 4-car Class 312 emus for the London Midland and Eastern regions. These sets hold the distinction of being the last 'slam door' sets constructed at the Works. An MBS vehicle for this build is seen taking shape in the New Build Shop.

A bodyside skeleton for a Taiwan export coach awaits marrying up with other fabrications to form a complete shell, in readiness for panelling and subsequent fitting out. At the far end of the Shop a high-density emu coach for BR can be seen.

These two illustrations show a Class 315 DMS under construction. The first, shows the skeleton framework being welded together from the non-driving end, and the window and door openings can be seen already present. The second view also shows a welder working on a skeleton frame, but this time a previously assembled roof section is being slowly manipulated into position.

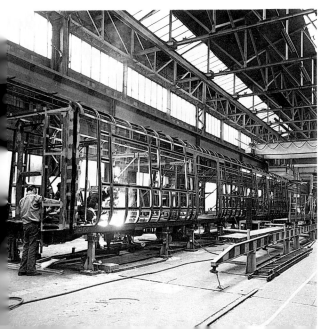

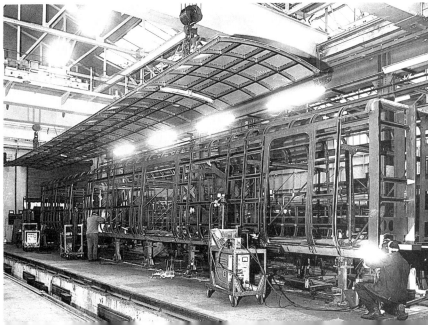

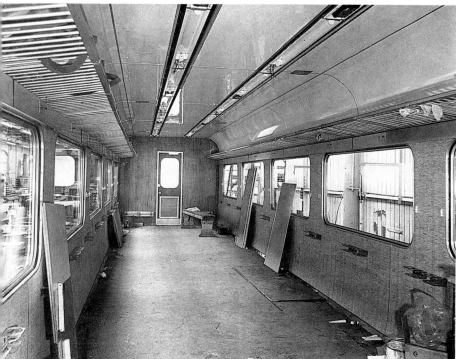

The export contract to supply stock to Taiwan was a considerable boost to the Works during the mid-1970s. The build was based on the highly successful BR Mk II design, but a number of refinements were incorporated to suit the customer's requirements. The upper illustration shows a nearly completed body shell, which has obvious differences to a similar BR type. The lower view, shows the interior of a Taiwan coach prior to fitting out. A very close resemblance between this and BR builds is apparent.

Both: Colin J. Marsden

A major part of all new build programmes involving electric multiple units is in the installation of traction and power collection equipment, with one section of the Finishing Shop being dedicated to traction purposes. In this view an electrician inspects a Class 315 pantograph which is in the process of installation. At this stage in the vehicle production cycle, no internal fittings would be installed.

Apart from the constructional undertaking, one of the most important briefs at York Works was the classified overhaul of loco-hauled stock. For this, one large building was set aside which could accommodate upwards of 30 vehicles at any one time. Mk II TSO No. E5162 is seen on accommodation stands while receiving a general overhaul on 5th February 1986.

Colin J. Marsden

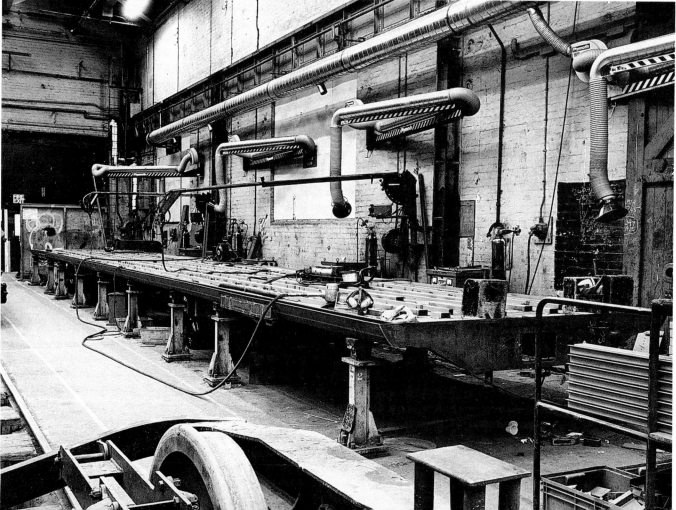

Although the number of Mk I coaches has decreased rapidly in recent years, when this photograph was taken in Spring 1986, classified attention to Mk Is was still evident, as demonstrated in this view of the Main Repair Shop with no fewer than five Mk I vehicles present.

Colin J. Marsden

In the mid-1980s the most important operation within the Works was fulfilling new build contracts, with during early 1986 the order books being almost filled to capacity. The first stage of building is the fabrication of vehicle underframes, this being carried out in the Frame Shop where special assembly jigs were provided. Here a Class 318 vehicle is seen in the very early stages of frame construction in February 1986.

Colin J. Marsden

Whilst the main underframes were formed in the Frame Shop, the vehicle roof and side panels were assembled in the New Build Shop. This illustration shows a Class 318 MS roof being formed. At the near end the lower roof section is where the pantograph was eventually installed.

Colin J. Marsden

In early 1986 the first of the Class 150/2 units took shape, this fleet eventually running to 85 members, being almost identical to the Class 150/1 type, except that end gangways were fitted, and some revision made to constructional methods. DMS(L) No. 52201 of unit No. 150201 is seen on the left, while one of the DTS vehicles for Class 317/2, No. 317368 is seen on the right.

Colin J. Marsden

A general view of the main New Build Shop, with various Class 317 cars on the right, while in the foreground, several already formed body panels are seen stored awaiting assembly. Throughout the Shop many overhead cranes and MonoRail lifting hooks were provided.

Colin J. Marsden

Once vehicle bodies were constructed the fitting out process began, this task lasting some four weeks, and saw the vehicle taken to a number of different Shops. Prior to any fitting out the completed body shell was primed to ensure that no possible corrosion damage caused by water or dampness could occur. A Class 317/2 MS is illustrated in the Paint Shop.

Colin J. Marsden

During the advanced stages of assembly, with all windows already installed and most technical equipment fitted, DTS No. 77215 of Class 317/2 No. 317364 is seen waiting to be lowered onto its bogies for final testing.

Colin J. Marsden

The internal fitting out of new vehicles was carried out on a flowline basis. This illustration shows eight Class 317/2 vehicles posed alongside the central fitting out platform, where all stores and cutting benches were provided.

Colin J. Marsden

As well as carrying out vehicle maintenance and assembly, large Shops were dedicated to the maintenance and assembly of component parts such as bogies. Here we see various all-steel Commonwealth bogies and the established B4 style being repaired.

Colin J. Marsden

In the mid-1980s, when BR was actively involved in the design for replacement stock for the ageing dmmu fleet, both BREL York and Metro-Cammell produced 3-car prototype sets. Although the original 'follow on' orders from these prototypes all went to BREL, however, all was not lost for Metro-Cammell as the company was eventually awarded a substantial contract to produce Class 156 'Super Sprinter' sets. Here we see the original BR 'Sprinter' car No. 55200 on one of the York traversers.

After individual vehicles were completed and testing carried out, 'sets' were formed. A further short testing period then followed. For diesel units this involved a 200 mile active run, before the units were transferred to their new home. The upper photograph shows a pair of Class 150/1 'Sprinters' Nos 150141 and 150142 awaiting despatch, while the lower view shows Class 317/2s Nos 317356 and 317357 in the yard. The set on the right is coupled to a matchwagon, as the stock is fitted with 'Tightlock' couplers and not compatible with locomotives.

Both: Colin J. Marsden

To provide stock for the Network SouthEast
"ThamesLink" service, connecting the Southern
Region with the London Midland main line, a fleet
of Class 319 units was built by BREL York. This
view shows the main Construction Shop with
various coaches under assembly.

Brian Morrison

The Class 319 construction programme, which
commenced in mid-1987, was initially for 46
units, however this was increased to 60. A Class
319 Driving Car is seen under construction at
York.

Brian Morrison

▶

After receiving its main assembly a Class 319
Driving Car stands in the Finishing Shop where all
details would have been installed. A fitter is seen
perched in the unglazed centre doorway whilst
attending to wiring.

Brian Morrison

▶

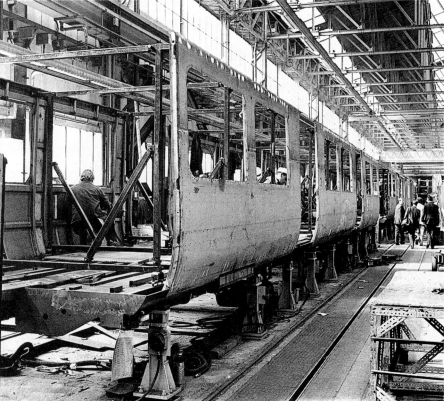

Furthering its association with the modernisation
of the railways' multiple unit fleets, York constructed the Class 321 25kV emus for Anglia and
London Midland Regions in 1988-89. The first of
the build, No. 321301 is seen with many of the
construction staff outside York Works on 15th
September 1988.

Brian Morrison

In an almost complete state, set No. 321304 is seen under construction at York during September 1988. With their streamlined front ends these units are some of the most distinctive in service on BR.
Brian Morrison

York Works Training School, built in 1962 provided craft trainees with twelve months off the job training, prior to entry into the main Works. The latest systems of training, meeting requirements of the Engineering Industry Training Board, were followed. The School usually accommodated some 60 trainees at one time.

Colin J. Marsden